ARCHITECTURE

OAB

Cover image: Pavilion in Sonaiet. Photo by Joan Guillamat

ARCHITECTURE

Office of
Architecture
in Barcelona

FERRATER & PARTNERS

Office of Architecture in Barcelona

Carlos Ferrater

This book represents a time for reflection since 1970. The document that follows attempts to define a new approach to the architectural project that is both personal and professional.

Until 2005, my studio carried out its work in a small office with just four or five employees. Occasionally we collaborated with other studios and contracted specialists to offer their expertise during design and construction phases.

The development of the Office of Architecture in Barcelona (OAB) grew out of these relationships. OAB was established in 2005 by Carlos Ferrater, Xavier Martí Galí and Lucia and Borja Ferrater as a collective platform informed by our past experiences. The early results of this new entity, including projects conceived and completed by the studio in the five years since its founding, are presented in this publication.

OAB draws on the collaborative nature of my previous studio, incorporating new ways of understanding the contributions of each team member to generate richer, more varied, prepared and flexible projects. The creation of this new platform attempts to tackle the challenges that contemporary architecture has raised in intellectual and social, technological and environmental spheres.

Inspired by the social nature of group work and the personal style of the studio's contributors, this book is organized into a collection of chapters; the projects and recently built works convey a willingness to work in different scenarios, expanding and enriching the range of propositions in the pursuit of new avenues of formal expression. The book covers the theoretical aspects of each project, focusing on innovation, research, and the application of new technologies. At the same time, as we explore each project's development, emphasis is placed on context, the building's objectives and the social roots of the architect's work.

It is important to remark the collaboration of young architects like Núria Ayala, as Director of Projects in OAB, and associated architects like the Studio of Alberto Peñín.

A series of circumstances led to the birth of this new platform and along the way we have maintained the position that each new project represents a different experience and requires a tailored approach. Furthermore, the platform is built on several basic tenets: embracing innovation and experimentation, conceptual flexibility, and a willingness to offer alternative architectural propositions.

Throughout the development of the publication, we must address what we have already learned and remember that the essence of the architect does not lie in language, delineation styles, or process methodologies. Rather, it lies in the architect's unique ability to respond to the conditions of the site and the city, to recognize the social complexity of program organization, to harness the use of light as a raw material of design – with its capacity to generate space and emotion – and to affect sensory perception through materiality. When these skills are harnessed and harmoniously combined, the architect can bring the architecture closer to future users and residents.

I will attempt to explain the circumstances that led to the formation of OAB. First came the decision from a group of young architects, members of my own family, who decided to turn the work of a studio into a collective experience.

Second, the new studio was conceptually enabled and strengthened through the development of a cohesive theoretical corpus, culled from the knowledge we gained from previous project experiences. This knowledge is compiled in Synchronizing Geometry, an exhibition that documents preparatory procedures for our projects. Our use of open and flexible complex geometries as instruments capable of probing the intellectual conditions and cultural history of places and landscapes allows us to create varied and pointed responses.

This instrumentation, from the use of geometry, shapes the organizational and programmatic framework while providing constructive mechanisms that make it possible to convert initial ideas and original concepts into constructed realities.

Following an invitation from the IIT (Illinois Institute of Technology), OAB exhibited documents and models that illustrate theoretical concepts, while arguing for different empirical approaches to architectural inquiries. Exhibited in the lobby of Mies van der Rohe's Crown Hall, the show has since been expanded with new documents and additional models of experimental projects. They are now exhibited in the Schools of Architecture in Barcelona and Madrid, the Bezalel Academy of Arts and Design, Jerusalem, Tel Aviv University, the Museum of Fine Arts Bilbao, Acquario di Roma and Minar Odasi Büyükkent Subesi of Istambul, among others. The roaming exhibition is continually updated, and will continue to travel to different institutions and universities worldwide.

The third circumstance came about from the importance and necessity of simultaneously designing both the architectural and structural solutions.

In almost all projects covered in Synchronizing Geometry, structure is understood as the spatial support of the project, sometimes the structural skeleton is even conceived as a final form of the construction. Thus the reinforced earth walls in the Botanical Garden of Barcelona, the "load bearing" membrane as an urban façade on the Mediapro building, the reinforced concrete sheet that fuses the shapes of the seafront Promenade in Benidorm, the topographic roof of the Science Park in Granada, or the light diaphragm on the roof of the Zaragoza- Delicias Intermodal Station, among other projects, have led us to establish a synchronous collaboration with Juan Calvo, an engineer, whose formation was closer to Jörg Schaich and a experience in large civil engineering works, particularly bridges and long-span structures, has given us the opportunity to incorporate our own solutions in to the engineering of the building.

We decided to situate the new studio in Barcelona city centre in the Eixample Cordà district, in Carrer Balmes and Còrsega, near Avinguda Diagonal, establishing activities in two different locations.

The first, on Carrer Balmes 145 is destined to house the professional structure and the second on Carrer Còrsega 254 is to accommodate cultural activities and academic research. This functional separation allows parallel developments while minimizing interference.

In Carrer Balmes the studio concentrates on initial ideas, models and drawings, the basic structure of the design projects, competitions and sometimes the technical solutions for these works. Here, we try to avoid those cumbersome and bureaucratic aspects that hinder and undermine the fragility of the creative process, encouraging collaboration with partner studios and connections with the work teams who develop the construction on-site, always directed by one of the main architects. This organization allows for greater agility, flexibility and interaction between teams.

The Gallery on Carrer Còrsega allows the organization of workshops and seminaries, receives groups of architects visiting Barcelona, and it's the exhibition space of our model collection, illustrating the moments of greatest creative tension of the projects.

It is also a documentation center that collects and codifies publications, monographs, brochures and mediadedicated to the work of the studio. The OAB gallery has also the imprint of Palimpsesto Ed., which publishes academic and cultural works related to the architecture praxis.

This working structure allows great flexibility, good relationships between members of the team and it facilitates the inclusion of issues unrelated to the world of architecture that help to enrich the project process.

Revisiting the Barcelona Botanical Garden 1989-1999-2009-2019

Carlos Ferrater

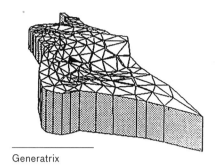

Generatrix

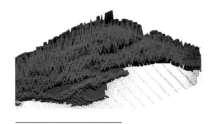

Vertex elevation

The Barcelona Botanical Garden is located on Montjuïc, between the castle and the Estadi Olímpic Lluís Companys, on a site with uneven terrain (altitude between 140 metres and 100 metres). Its shape is reminiscent of an amphitheatre facing the northwest and has an area of about 14 hectares. For years it has been a municipal waste landfill that has been converted into one of the largest green spaces in the city. It offers magnificent views over the Llobregat delta, the Olympic Ring and much of the metropolitan area of Barcelona, with the mountains of the Garraf massif and the Sierras de Collserola and Marina as a backdrop.

The most immediate reference is the Historic Botanical Garden, founded in 1930 by Dr. Pius Font i Quer in the quarries of La Foixarda, Montjuïc and reopened to the public in October 2003. The need to build entrances to the new Olympic facilities in 1986, seriously affected it. This situation helped push forward the proposal to build a new botanical garden in Barcelona, which would house a new building for the Botanical Institute and its collections. It would become a reference centre for the preservation of Mediterranean flora.

The Garden project employs a triangular grid structure fractured with concrete paths that adapt to the terrain and arrange the routes, the construction and infrastructure, while allowing the harmonious distribution of vegetation units.

The Garden displays a representation of the flora from regions around the world with a Mediterranean climate. Mediterranean vegetation is considered one of the richest in species diversity. It is estimated that only 1.7 percent of the Earth's land surface has a Mediterranean climate, but those regions account for 20 percent of the world's flora and more than half are endemic. Today, Mediterranean vegetation is severely threatened mainly due to human activity. For this reason, the Garden has two main objectives: to contribute to the preservation of plant species and to create awareness, increasing public respect for nature and the value of biodiversity.

The Mediterranean basin (between 30° and 45°N latitude) is not the only region with a Mediterranean climate. There are other areas of the planet, located at the same latitude in the northern hemisphere or an equivalent latitude in the southern hemisphere, which also have this climate. These areas include south and southwest Australia (between 27° and 37° S latitude), the south of South Africa (between 30° and 35° S latitude), central Chile (between 30° and 37° S latitude) and eastern California (between 30° and 42° N latitude). Together they form the Mediterranean biome, a set of remote plant and animal communities far apart in terms of space but with similar characteristics due to climatic similarities.

The floral richness of these areas and the similarity of their plants and landscapes are the main source of inspiration for the Barcelona Botanical Garden.

It's been 20 years since 1989 when an international design competition to build a new botanical garden in the mountain of Montjuïc was held.

The proposals had to be developed by interdisciplinary teams consisting of architects, landscape architects, botanists, biologists, engineers, etc. In the failure of a unanimous agreement by the jury, the remark by Maria Aurèlia Capmany on the fractal and Mediterranean condition of our proposal played in our favour, a view that was the deciding factor for the jury, declaring us the winner of that competition.

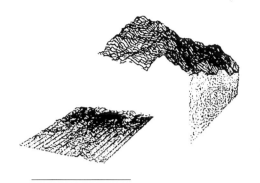

Fractal islands

It has been more than 10 years since 1999, the year in which construction of the garden was completed and the first plantings were carried out. First abstract proposal to superimpose a grid on the land, to work scale-free and to incorporate a few certain constructive mechanisms, operating on sustainable principles, has allowed us to create a new landscape on that landfill. The network of paths, walls and interstitial spaces, today forms the shape and decoration of the gardens, while on the contrary, the vegetation and plant communities today make up the scientific structure of the garden. The original grid has been visually diminished but it still remains as an intrinsic and natural order of a new landscape. At the end of the intervention, the boundary between natural and artificial, between structure and ornament, has gradually become undetectable.

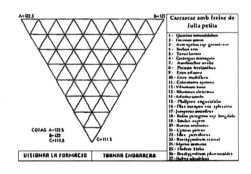

Plant community programme

In recent years, a series of new additions, further expansion of the network of paths, plantations in the areas of Australia, California and the Mediterranean as well as new infrastructures such as the multipurpose outdoor space, have completed the former intervention.

It is for all the above mentioned reasons that 20 years since that first competition and 10 since the construction of the garden, it is appropriate to revisit and review those principles, as well as the method for approaching a project and how to proceed in terms of construction.

Fractal construction of the landscape

The first consideration was how to achieve a project argument in which the actual site provided the construction guidelines, placing emphasis on the morphological and topographical conditions of the new landscape.

The second consideration involved the structure of the new garden, which had to include the Mediterranean flora as well as those from other homoclimatic areas, California and part of Japan in the northern hemisphere and in the symmetrical parallel of the southern hemisphere, a part of Chile, South Africa and a small region of the Australian coast. The layout of the new garden would be based on botanical and ecosystem issues, as well as the use of the convergence concept of plant morphology, becoming a tool of high scientific value and a part of the future of twenty-first century botanical gardens.

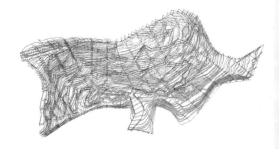

First handmade sketch

The synthesis of these two intentions would only be possible if we were to have an instrument capable of promoting dialogue and the joint work between the different disciplines, an impossible task in the early days of the project. This is how the idea of a triangular grid on the site emerged. The grid would have to adapt to all unevenness, fraying at the edges and increases or decreases in the surface according to the varying topographic slope. The guidelines of the triangular grid would follow the three main directions of the contour lines, thus ensuring that two vertices of each triangle were at the same level, slope line 0. Other subdivisions of the grid in accordance with the concepts of accessibility, plantation, etc. would maintain the same structure.

Grid model built in steel fiber

General plan

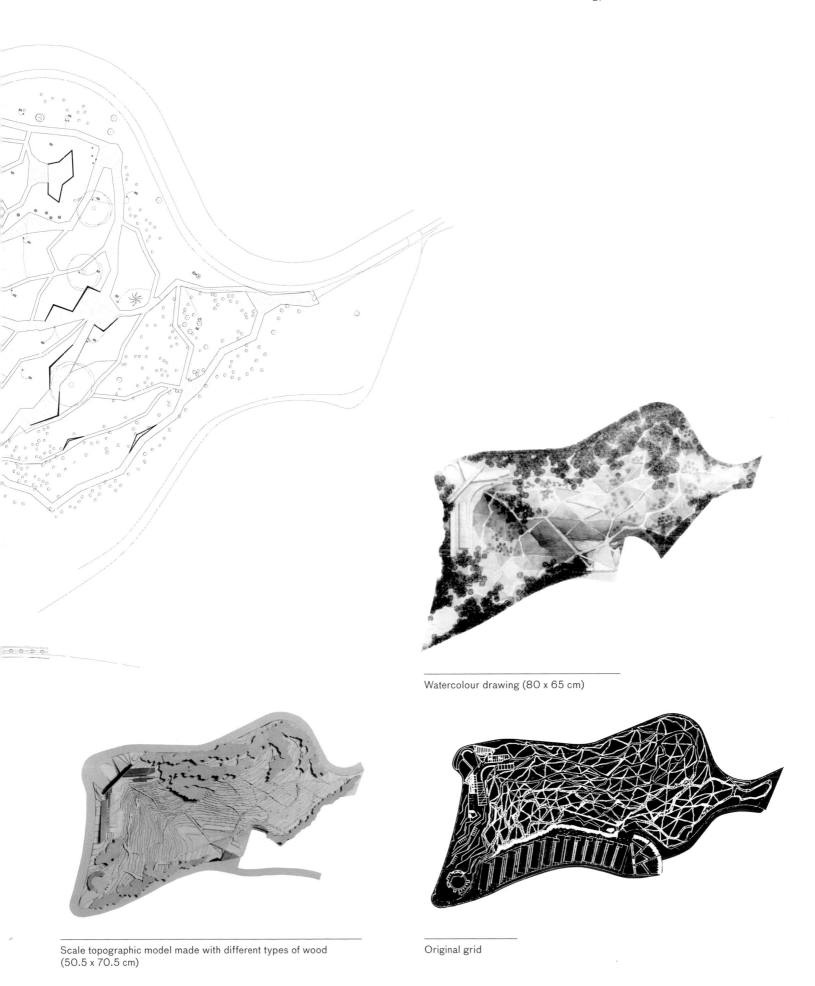

Watercolour drawing (80 x 65 cm)

Scale topographic model made with different types of wood
(50.5 x 70.5 cm)

Original grid

The Garden offers collections of Mediterranean plants distributed according to geographical areas (Australia, Chile, California, South Africa and the Mediterranean basin) and, in turn, grouped according to the landscapes that they form in nature. These groupings, called phyto-episodes (plant communities) are the exhibition and management units of the Botanical Garden. There are currently 87 phyto-episodes. The forests communities are located in the highest areas and those dominated by shrub-like plants can be found in the central and lower areas.

Australia. The Australian Mediterranean region, with 700,000km^2, is the second largest (accounting for just over 20 percent of the biome). It is formed by two separate sectors, located in the southwest and south of the continent. There are some 8,000 known species, 75 percent of which are endemisms. The climate is Mediterranean with some tropical influence due to the proximity of the ocean monsoons, so the summer drought is not as rigorous as in our Mediterranean area, but even so the frequency of fires is high.

In the Australian area of the Garden, in addition to its characteristic Mediterranean flora, warm flora from the southwest of the continent are also cultivated (the states of Victoria and New South Wales). Both the tree-like and shrub-like plants are dominated by a large number of species from few families, such as the mimosa (Acacia), Myrtaceae (Eucalyptus, Melaleuca, Callistemon) and Proteaceae (Hakea, Banksia, Grevillea).

Chile. The Mediterranean area of Chile is a narrow coastal strip of about 100 kilometres corresponding to the region of central Chile. Its area is 140,000km^2 and it represents less than 5% of the biome. Climatically, it has a rather cool character marked by the influence of the ocean, with plenty of coastal fog. There are some 2,400 known species, 23 percent of which are endemic. An important ecological feature of this area is the historical absence of fire, and a marked presence of herbivores, in particular camelids (llamas and guanacos). There is, therefore, an abundance of thorny bushes and plants are not adapted to fire.

The Chilean Mediterranean area has a variety of sclerophyllous landscapes (plants with stiff and rigid leaves), with woodland and shrub formations including the sclerophyll forest to the coastal scrubland, and including "el espinal" or spiny hillside scrublands. Many Chilean plants have the names of Iberian plants as early settlers compared them to those they were familiar with.

California. The Mediterranean area of California occupies a narrow coastal strip from Cape Blanco, in the United States, to Punta Baja, Mexico, with the centre more or less in San Francisco. To the east, the strip extends about 100 or 200 kilometres inland. Despite its small size (about 10 percent of the total biome), it is the area with the largest continuous expanses of unchanged Mediterranean landscapes. There are some 4,300 known species, 35 percent of which are endemisms. Climatically, the seasonality is very pronounced as 85 percent of the rainfall is concentrated

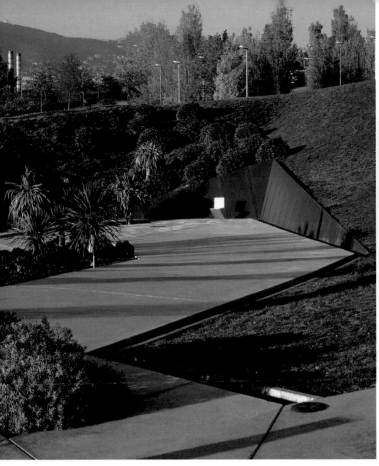

in the winter. The summer droughts are very severe but the coastal fog partly relieves this contrast.

South Africa. The South African Mediterranean area is the smallest of all and represents just 3 percent of the biome. There are some 8,550 known species of which 68 percent are endemic. Rain is most intense in the cold season however it is never very abundant. Moreover, due to the summer influence of tropical monsoons, there is no completely dry season. Despite the presence of the Mediterranean climate at the two ends of the African continent, the flora of this region has few genera in common with the Mediterranean basin. The diversity of soils, climate and topography, together with geographical isolation and the recurrence of fires, have led to very high diversity and to

the proportion of endemic and rare species making it, along with the southwest of Australia, the highest of the Mediterranean areas and one of the richest in the world.

In the Garden, the Mediterranean area of The Cape, the subtropical territories of Karoo and Savannah and temperate zones of the south-eastern forests are represented.

Mediterranean Basin.

The quintessential Mediterranean area is the Mediterranean basin, i.e. the lands surrounding the Mediterranean Sea. It stretches across European, Asian and African territories and has an area of 2,300,000km². There are some 25,000 known species, of which 50 percent are endemic. Mediterranean flora has many solutions to adapt to the ecological factors that have influenced

its evolution. Rigid and persistent leaves to resist the dry summer, spikes, thorns and toxic substances to defend themselves against herbivores, low plants in the form of a pin cushion, or shrubs that lose their leaves in summer to reduce transpiration. The great capacity for the regeneration of plants in the Mediterranean basin (five times higher than those of the California chaparral, which is the area it most resembles) clearly shows the importance of centuries of human intervention. Humans, with the help of ploughs, fire and cattle have profoundly shaped Mediterranean plants and landscapes.

The flora of the Mediterranean basin has been distributed in the Garden in four bio-geographical sub-regions: eastern Mediterranean (between Italy and the

Caucasus), western Mediterranean (Iberian Peninsula and Balearic Islands and Tyrrhenian), northern Africa (from Morocco to Tunisia) and the Canary Islands.

The Botanical Institute of Barcelona is located within the Garden, it a research centre with a long tradition in Catalonia, which maintains the main scientific collections created in the country for more than three centuries. The current building, opened in 2003, includes an exhibition hall open to the public, where you can visit the Cabinet of Natural History. The Salvador Museum was the first museum open to the public in Barcelona.

Text taken from the *Col·lecció de Parcs i Jardins de l'AMB*

Barcelona Botanical Institute
for the Higher Council of Scientific Research

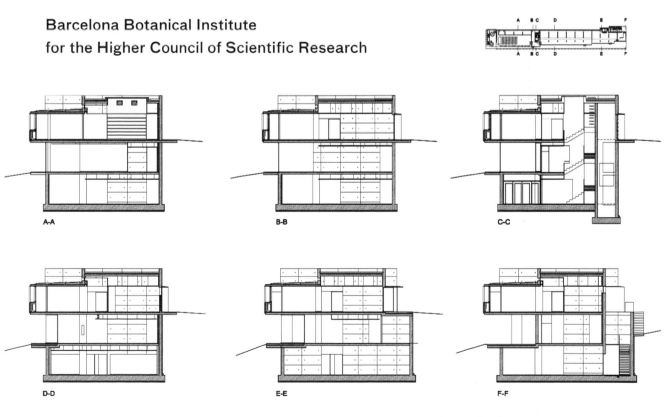

A-A

B-B

C-C

D-D

E-E

F-F

0 2 4 6 8 10 20

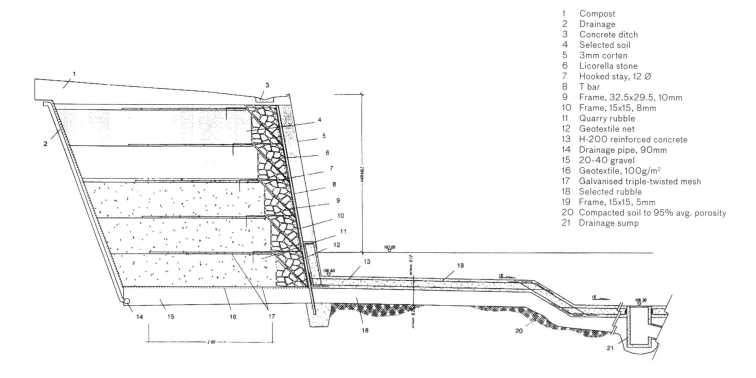

1   Compost
2   Drainage
3   Concrete ditch
4   Selected soil
5   3mm corten
6   Licorella stone
7   Hooked stay, 12 Ø
8   T bar
9   Frame, 32.5x29.5, 10mm
10 Frame, 15x15, 8mm
11 Quarry rubble
12 Geotextile net
13 H-200 reinforced concrete
14 Drainage pipe, 90mm
15 20-40 gravel
16 Geotextile, 100g/m²
17 Galvanised triple-twisted mesh
18 Selected rubble
19 Frame, 15x15, 5mm
20 Compacted soil to 95% avg. porosity
21 Drainage sump

Section of reinforced wall

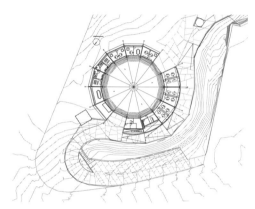

The Botanic Garden is a constantly changing project where extensions such as the amphitheatre, the bonsai display, the California forests and the new upper access building have been developed over the years.

One of these new contributions has been the Maintenance Building constructed on the initial circular design. It brings together gardening work areas, changing rooms, dining rooms and toilets, as well as germplasm banks and classrooms for staff training, all of them developed around a courtyard surrounded by a canopy supported by pillars that also act as lights. This encourages communication between the different employees working in the building: gardeners, horticulturists, researchers and administrative and security staff.

Residential architecture and the city

Carlos Ferrater

This chapter addresses the issue of multifamily housing, showcasing two buildings simultaneously over time that respond to different typological programmes, small apartments in the case of the Vertix Diagonal building, and larger-scale housing in the M3 building in Plaza Lesseps. Two spaces in transformation in the city of Barcelona, the first in the recently created Diagonal, and the second in an area that has undergone many changes in recent times.

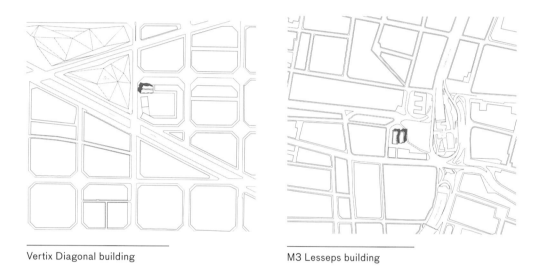

Vertix Diagonal building   M3 Lesseps building

Both buildings pose questions that deal with the construction of the city, defining urban areas from the architectural project, while raising substantive issues on typological diversity and the construction of flexible and lightweight façades that encompass sustainability, environmental control and Mediterranean traditions.

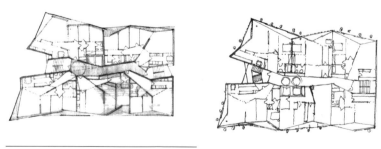

Sketch for Vertix Diagonal building

Carlos Ferrater Xavier Martí Galí

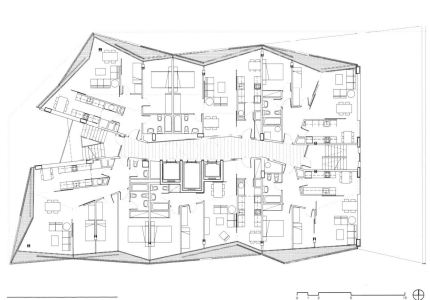

Vertix Diagonal building

In Barcelona's new Diagonal, opposite the Central Park designed by Jean Nouvel at the end of the north arm of the block, there is a residential building with a twofold purpose, first as the façade of the open block of the Cerdá Plan, and secondly, that of an autonomous piece.

Six apartments per floor organised around a zigzagged corridor that links the two vertical circulation cores and designs the communal space and light towards the exterior.

The houses have intermediate spaces that are obtained on the basis of the winding, different levels of the façade, where the sliding blinds are arranged on the interior and exterior thereby maintaining privacy and light control but at the same time helping to create open spaces that link the exterior and the interior, making the separation walls of the homes unnecessary.

The configuration of the building allows for a variety of typologies. This versatility is reflected in the development of 1, 2 and 3 bedroom apartments on one floor.

The dimensions are defined by the treatment of the outer skin. Black-painted steel ribs form the skin of the building, while solving the intertwined form of the metal slats and interior glass around the perimeter of the façade. Fractures in the skin are found in spaces housing stairs.

Typical floor plan

Longitudinal section

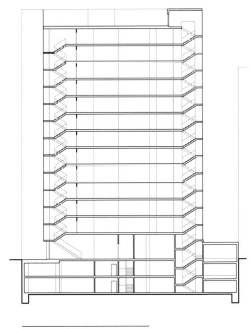

The projects presented in this chapter experiment with the intermediate space that is formed at the boundary between the exterior and interior areas of the home. The mobile or fixed shutter elements help to create a place that acts as a climate filter, regulating the level of privacy and solar control, creating spaces that become an extension of the house, something that José Antonio Coderch de Sentmenat experimented with when he built houses for fishermen in 1955, on Paseo de Juan de Borbón, in Barceloneta, opposite the port of Barcelona.

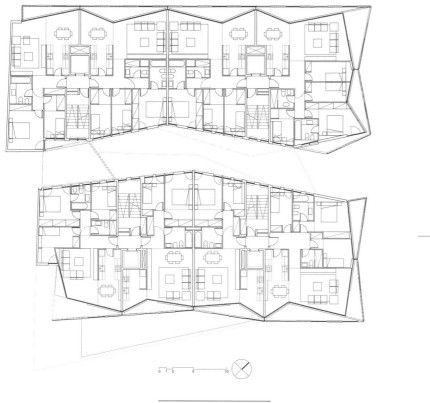

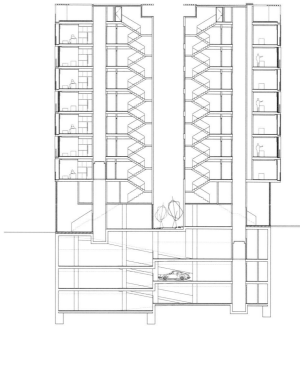

Typical floor plan

Cross section

Carlos Ferrater   Lucía Ferrater

Lesseps Metro-3 Building

This building adheres to the specific volume criteria outlined it in the city of Barcelona's new metropolitan plans. The opening of a new passage and the expansion of the Avinguda del Hospital Militar shape the physical framework and regulations of the intervention.

The project proposes the division of the building into two separate volumes with an open space as a continuous courtyard. This decision makes full use of the space with lights reaching 2.5 metres, allowing all the rooms to be naturally ventilated.

The open space setting of the building between blocks in a longitudinal direction, allows for a shift in the corner that contains the double wall of the building, emphasising the fracture volume.

Access to the premises on the ground floor is created by the space between the blocks and also from the streets. The car park is divided into three basement floors accessed via a ramp next to the party wall with access from Carrer Riera de Vallcarca, this being the lowest point of the site. There are four different entrances to the apartments, two located on the north façade and two on the south.

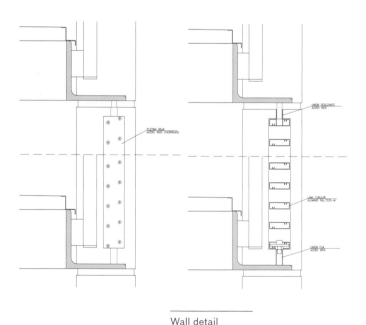

Wall detail

The façades offer a set of fixed and sliding metal shutters that open and close the terraces and allow for better integration of indoor-outdoor spaces, regulating daylight. These shutters, made of stainless steel, transverse tubular crossbeams lacquered in pearl grey. They are framed by fine steel railings forming a grid where the vertical bars create a rhythm and the horizontal beams refine the pace of the framework. This latticework façade, along with the interior glass planes, wind around the entire perimeter creating interstitial spaces, transition areas between the city and the interior inhabited space, a heritage of Mediterranean architecture.

The building, next to the Joan Fuster library, has been constructed as a symbol of the new Plaça Lesseps in Barcelona.

Carlos Ferrater

Xavier Martí Galí

Alberto Peñín

Twelve Houses in Calle Fernando Poo, Barcelona

Located in the old fabric of Poble Nou, at a transitional point between the historic axis of María Agulló, the Rambla de Poble Nou, and the approaches to the beach, the project responds to this dual condition. On the one hand, Calle Fernando Poo reasserts the traditional typology of the house, two-story housing that makes no secret of its individuality to the street. On the other, the corner, empty but with well-defined arrises that stand out against the sky, looks out at the city of Barcelona with its animated flux of inhabitants and visitors who flow beachwards.

In Calle San Francesc the typological solution insists on the animation of the ground floors as a founding element of the social control of the city. A simple system of entrances avoids elevators and extends the street towards the interior of the houses and communal spaces. The collective constructs the city and organizes through-dwellings on the ground floor and duplex dwellings on the first. The corner is resolved with a T-shaped dwelling that opens onto the inner courtyard and an empty space that proposes a fresh interruption on Calle Fernando Poo.

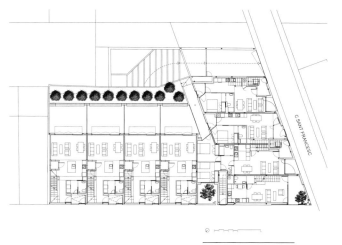

Ground floor

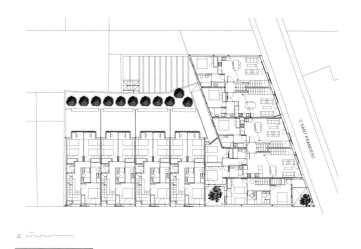

First floor

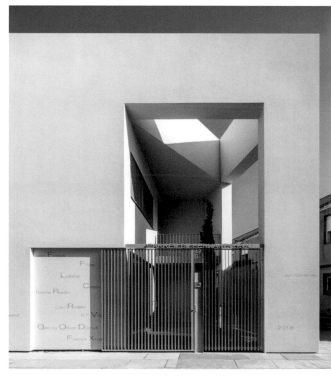

Multifamily building at Calle Cartagena 312, Barcelona

On the right side of the Ensanche, only meters from Hospital de Sant Pau and Avenida Gaudí (Sagrada Familia), a building with a 6.14 m façade and a depth of 24 m, the habitual dimensions in Barcelona's grid system due to the fact that the regulations did not permit the construction of high-rise buildings (ground floor, mezzanine and 5 further floors) on lots measuring less than 6 m.

The project is resolved with business premises on the ground and mezzanine floors and one through apartment per floor on each of the other five stories.

An exercise in "infill" habitual in our studio. This building takes account of the experience with mechanized carpentries in the building at Calle Rosselló 257, next to Paseo de Gracia, by organizing big frames with pivoting windows with a vertical and horizontal axis, and a running sill in glass blocks.

With such walling one obtains extremely good illumination of the interior space as well as highly effective ventilation of the rooms on the façade, added to which one solves the darkening of the interior by means of blinds on the inside of the room, something that facilitates the cleaning of all the glass surfaces of the façade.

Typical floor plan

Mobility Infrastructures
Intermodality

Carlos Ferrater

Zaragoza-Delicias Intermodal Station

The international design competition for the Zaragoza-Delicias Intermodal Station, which the Ministry of Development convened among a selection of Spanish and foreign architects including Norman Foster, Santiago Calatrava, Ricardo Bofill, Richard Rogers, Rafael Moneo and Ábalos & Herreros, allowed us to work in and explore a field that until a few decades ago was exclusively reserved for the world of transport infrastructure engineering.

The TWA terminal in New York and the Foster Dulles terminal in Washington, both projects designed by the Finnish architect Eero Saarinen were milestones in airport architecture and in recent times we have witnessed extraordinary airport projects designed by architects such as Stansted by Norman Foster or Kansai airport by Renzo Piano.

Working with large flows of people, mobility limitations and Intermodal connections between different transport modes are all fundamental points:
High speed trains, buses and coaches, large changeover areas and car parks for public and private vehicles demand the effective management of changing between different modes of transport making the process more fluid, more agile and quicker.

This was one of the challenges raised by the Zaragoza-Delicias Intermodal train station, a city in a blurred territory, with the high speed train it has become an important node located 75 minutes from Barcelona and Madrid and in the future Valencia and Bilbao making it a key station for connections with Europe. This meant that the design of the station had to allow for a quick and efficient connection from all means of transport to the high speed train. For this reason the station is equipped with double arrivals and departure halls as well as a transfer hall that lies below the tracks, although it is assisted by natural light and in a few minutes via remote-doors allows private car users, public transport, coaches or trains to access the high-speed trains. This layout is similar to how an airport operates; a typological experimentation for new twenty-first century stations.

Delicias station is structured as a major hub of growth in the city as was El Pilar in its day. Delicias station helps to merge two districts, it is the backbone for the Expo towards the river Ebro and it has become a nucleus for the services sector and installations, which are all located around the large 40,000m² structure (equivalent to the size of eight football fields). The station has a roof suspended by large arches and a tetrahedron mesh that offers natural light, good acoustics and a good level of environmental comfort while retaining the spatiality of the traditional station.

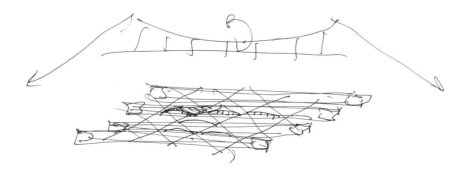

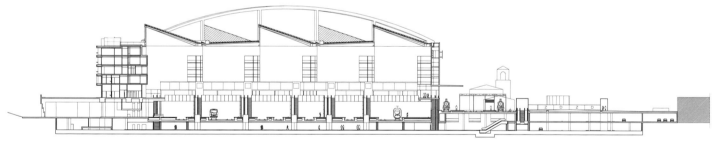

Cross section

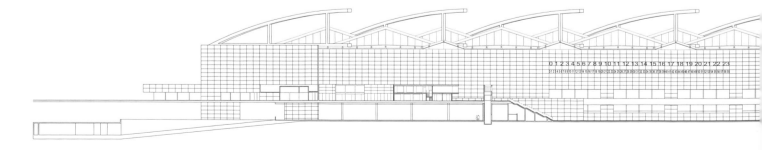

Longitudinal section

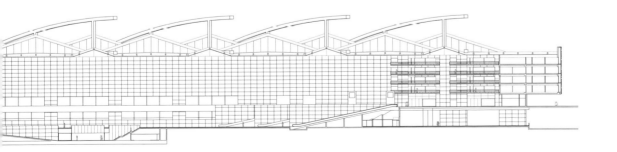

Intermodal Building at Barcelona Airport

After the experience in Zaragoza and being named finalists of the competition for the new terminal at Barcelona Airport, we decided, along with Ramon Sanabria and J.M. Casadevall, to set up a studio to develop projects in the field of transport infrastructure collaborating with various engineers. This has allowed us to carry out several projects in the airport of Barcelona such as the multimodal building, which we are currently working on, the façade of the new city airport and the Line 9 station at terminals 1 and 2. We are also working on the construction of Murcia airport after winning the competition organised by the Ministry of Infrastructure in 2008. Though perhaps to date, our greatest achievement has been the completion of the Intermodal building at Barcelona airport. The project has a neutral and opaque façade built with sleek aluminium profiles and the frieze by Joan Miró put the finishing touch to the enclosure between the old terminals A and B.

The building, an independent volume with glass skin on its four faces provides the gradual fusion of natural and artificial light by giving this new space a floating and apparently empty sensation even though the building is full of travellers.

Both the train station in Zaragoza, which earned the 2004 Brunell award, and the Intermodal building for the airport of Barcelona that earned the Flight International Award, raise questions about generic space. A station that becomes a micro indoor city where hotels, restaurants, office buildings, convention centres, shops or cultural activities, transmits a hybrid co-existence between the traditional public space and generic space advocated by Rem Koolhaas.

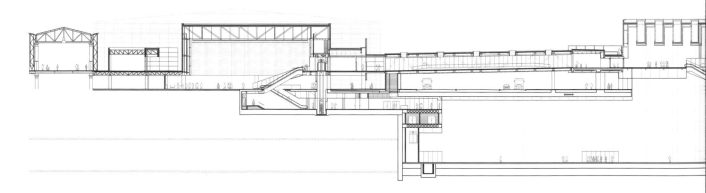

Longitudinal section

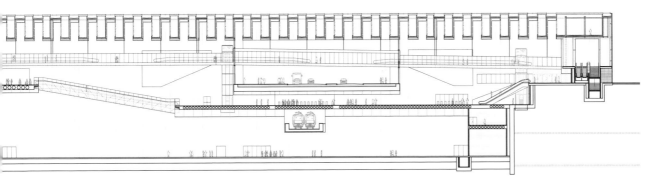

Rediscovering the <u>Eixample</u> morphology

Joan Busquets

The development of the Eixample Cerdà has become a laboratory for the evolution of architectural and urban forms.

We could say that the special contrast between the geometric rigidity of the Cerdà Plan and complexity of the geographical order of the "Llano de Barcelona" – formed by a system of roads, drains and properties – resulted in the morphological development of the Eixample, which at first sight seemed contradictory, but perhaps it is one of the reasons for the great spatial richness and diversity of its built-up and functional system.

It is common knowledge that the initial hypothesis of Cerdà to reserve much of the centre of the blocks as free and collective spaces was immediately overturned after its approval due to the increasing need to fill these spaces for industrial and large services. This initial proposal has been solved by recent activities, such as the new city ordinance of 1985 to free up the centre of the block for landscaped areas and, in some cases the block's courtyard has been reserved for public use.

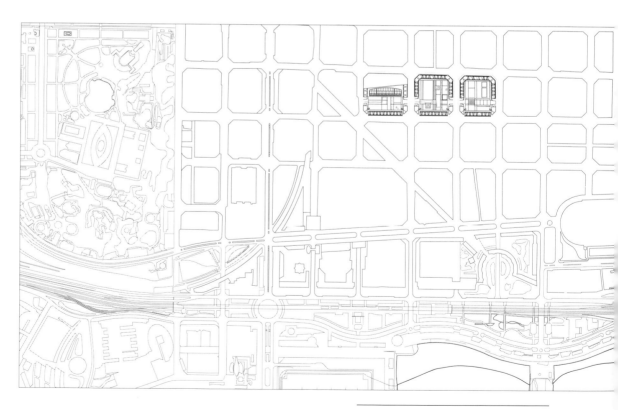

Three blocks in the Eixample, 1992

The development of Eixample over more than 150 years has consolidated a model of the closed block building, concentrated in the membrane of the block by establishing two well-defined situations: streets and corners. This has established a fairly constant system that different generations of architects have gradually used less frequently with many different stylistic hypotheses and programmes. As we celebrated the 150th anniversary of the Cerdà plan at the exhibition in the CCCB, we tried to investigate this hypothesis of mapping relevant examples following those two situations: either in a line i.e. following a street, or on a corner, i.e. solving the encounter between perpendicular streets. This exercise tests the richness of this typological laboratory i.e. the Eixample, in which it is clear that the stylistic conditions are nothing more than an accompaniment in regards to other crucial dimensions such as the insertion of the functional programme and/or the width of the plot on which the architecture is developed.

This recent research reveals the series of proposals by Carlos Ferrater and his team in the formation of a universe of typological proposals of great interest in both the situations mentioned above: whether "corner" or "line" that following the tradition already established by the MBM office in the sixties. These efforts are of great value because they are limited to private promotion operations and therefore are rarely given to research projects involving any risk. Several proposals for in line buildings and especially corner decomposition forces are particularly praiseworthy as in most cases they are infill operations within the existing structure and therefore subject to the residual logic of some of these plots.

Joan Busquets is Professor of Urban Planning Design in Harvard Graduate School of Design

Semi-open blocks with houses inside

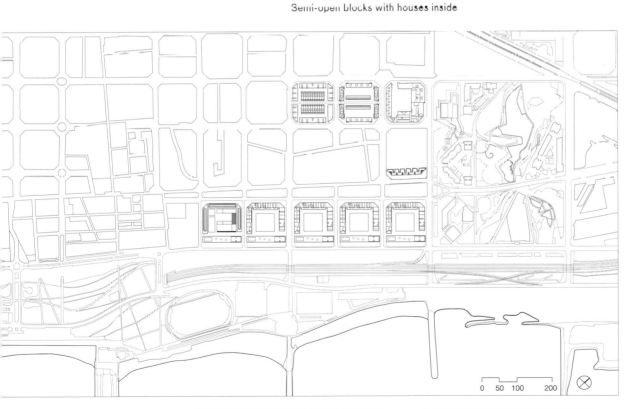

Five blocks in the seafront, 2010   Regesa social housing, 1998

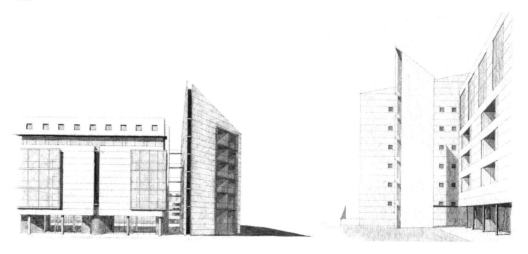

But undoubtedly the team's reflection on the Eixample is particularly interesting when dealing with the definition of new morphologies, for projects that have had the opportunity to present the architectural definition of several entire blocks. This is where taking another glance at the Cerdà project has led to some new dimensions. In fact these are new morphological interpretations already underway, such as, the second Olympic Village in Poble Nou or the Five Blocks on the Seafront.

In either case, the Ferrater team attempts to provide specific solutions for the fact that a project can become involved in a plot larger than that of the architectural site itself and can face up to the logic of the peripheral building and interior space of the block with new commitments.

The first case seeks to rediscover the block courtyard as the centre of the ensemble, producing an aggregate of three blocks that can have their own independent use even though they respond to a logic that allows for a unitary interpretation: To a certain extent, here they seem to recover the start of some passages that intersect and connect several blocks in central Eixample. Within this morphological concept, architecture seeks ways to create singular groups and the typological research is based on interesting principles of constructive rationality. On the other hand, exploration goes from encouraging the "line" of the building to addressing where the corners meet.

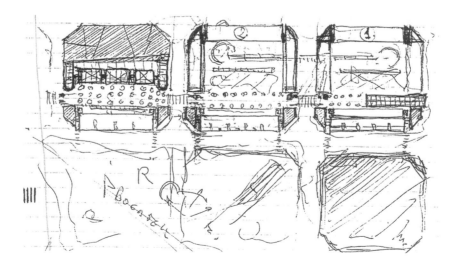

For the Five Blocks on the Seafront, the research is different. Once again, the idea that the closed block must include the perception of an interior courtyard is explored but the commitment lies in distinguishing the front of the block, which is the sea front. This is carried out to formulate a composition that goes beyond the individuality of each block and supports a multi-block composition that plays with large visual seafronts and the possibility that some more unique uses formalise the face of these spaces. This exercise seems to introduce the hybrid block solution as a way of tackling the problem of the singular points. New higher corners, which are now front pieces, let these buildings stand out without turning them into individual pieces, thus drawing attention to the complex.

We should add that the long periods of testing carried out by the Ferrater team on the Eixample verifies the enormous adaptability of the geometric conditions of the blocks proposed by Cerdà. It also demonstrates the team's unwavering commitment to continue to innovate and show how new programmes should come up with new typological answers. Above all we must be concerned about how the different decomposition of a block can introduce different compositional forms from which special morphological commitments are outlined. Despite the individuality of these commitments they continue to maintain a high level of consistency with the organisation of the monumental typology of which the Eixample is a historical legacy.

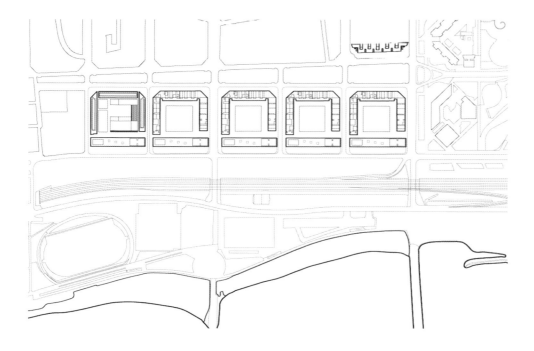

Eixample Cerdà– Passeig de Gràcia

The Eixample Cerdà has been a testing ground and an endless urban research laboratory for many architects. Its large size and its subtle breaks from the rigidity of a geometrical design has enabled us to interpret different rules for the same board game over 150 years, its different typological, constructive and formal solutions have constituted a high value urban façade with outstanding contributions such as the famous "Illa de la Discòrdia" or synthesis projects from the abstraction such as the façade of *El Noticiero Universal* building by J.M. Sostres.

The urban transformation of Barcelona started in the 80s with the fledgling democracy that allowed our studio to develop a set of project propositions and urban and architecture-based jobs as they worked on the shape and size of the roof at the same time as the interior space of the island creating it as a negative space. Without breaking the basic scheme of the traditional block, issues were addressed, such as buildable depth that would allow for accessible floors and cross ventilation, the permeability of the ground floor linking the road network and the landscaped interiors, the restoration of the terrace roofs as semi-public areas and providing orientation to the block and highlighting the planes and the chamfered corners. This led us to construct an image of cloistered and open interiors through the passages, diagonal perforations and paths that link the different blocks.

For example the project for the 3 blocks in the "Eixample Marítim del Poble Nou" in 1992 or the truncated blocks in the extension of Avda. Diagonal, a result of the consultation-tender planned by the City Council, or the new block created between the streets Ramón Turró and Llull. And in particular the urban proposal, also after an international competition for the Five Blocks on the Seafront in Barcelona, where for the first time a group of blocks from the Cerdà plan was erected in front of the sea. The collaborative work of the architecture critic and historian J.M. Montaner was of great value for the resolution of the majority of these projects.

Alongside these interventions, important for their urban transcendence and size, our studio has experimented with pieces of architecture of different sizes in other locations of Barcelona over the last few years. Such as buildings between party walls, those in the streets Balmes, Còrsega, València, or Gran Vía among others, or the more complex intervention in the *Block in Fort Pienc* by Lucía Ferrater with buildings in the streets Alí Bei, Roger de Flor and Nàpols around an interior landscaped island following the old Carretera d'Horta and organised around a small community centre. Although some of the chamfered corner proposals such as Urgell-Sepúlveda or the Casp-Bruc are currently under construction.

Special mention should be given to the rehabilitation carried out on Passeig de Gràcia, both for the quality and centrality of this urban street and for the extraordinary cultural legacy from previously carried out interventions, from modernism, with works of Gaudí, Puig i Cadafalch or Domènech i Muntaner, to valuable environmental and constructive rehabilitation or buildings from the second half of the twentieth century built by architects like Galindo, Tous and Moragas or Fargas.

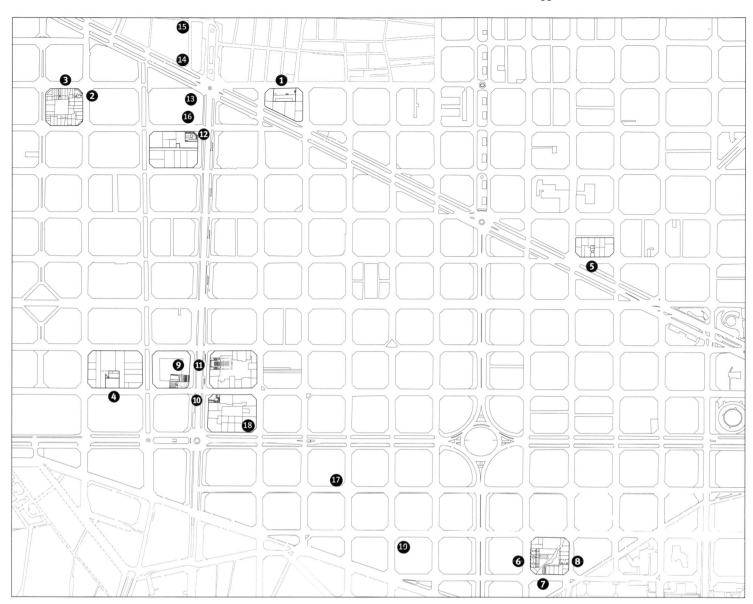

Since our first involvement in the old Cinema Fémina, which ceased to exist after a fire, we have rehabilitated the Passeig de Gràcia sector with an original typological proposal while recovering the façade in Carrer Diputació carried out by Moragas, connecting both volumes to "La Unión y el Fénix Español" building which forms the chamfer.

The complete rehabilitation, along with Lucía Ferrater and Joan Guibernau, of the former BASF Building on the chamfered corner of Rosselló with Passeig de Gràcia or the proposal of a new floor plan for the chamfered corner of Diputació-Passeig de Gràcia, carried out by Xavier Martí and Juan Trias de Bes, that Llàtzer Moix baptised "La Pedrera of the 21st century", is complemented by the refurbishment of the former Central Hispano Bank transforming it into the new Mandarin Oriental Hotel in collaboration with Juan Trias de Bes.

All these actions and projects have enabled us to understand the importance of taking on the complex cultural heritage, as well as recognising and respecting, the rich morphology, acting as a medium, of the Eixample in Barcelona.

1 Còrsega 254
2 Balmes 145
3 Còrsega 348
4 Diputació 239–247
5 València 381
6 Roger de Flor 78
7 Alí Bei 57 (Interior)
8 Nàpols 89–91
9 Passeig de Gràcia 23 / Diputació 259
10 Passeig de Gràcia 30
11 Passeig de Gràcia 38–40
12 Passeig de Gràcia 99
13 Passeig de Gràcia 105
14 Passeig de Gràcia 111
15 Passeig de Gràcia 125
16 Rosselló 257
17 Casp 35 / Bruc 31
18 Gran Via 619-621
19 Ausiàs March 34

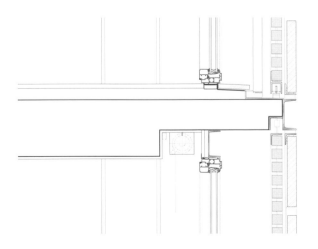

Balmes 145

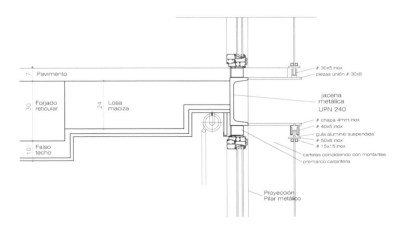

València 381

7　Pavimento

30　Forjado reticular　　24　Losa maciza

10　Falso techo

⌀ 30x5 inox
piezas unión ⌀ 30x8

jacena metálica
UPN 240

⌀ chapa 4mm inox
⌀ 40x5 inox
guía aluminio suspendida
⌀ 50x8 inox
⌀ 15x15 inox
cartelas coincidiendo con montantes
premarco carpintería

Proyección
Pilar metálico

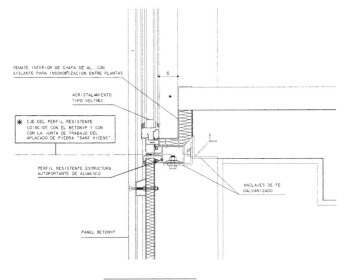

REMATE INTERIOR DE CHAPA DE AL..CON
AISLANTE PARA INSONORIZACION ENTRE PLANTAS

ACRISTALAMIENTO
TIPO VELTHEC

✳ EJE DEL PERFIL RESISTENTE
COINCIDE CON EL BETONYP Y CON
CON LA JUNTA DE TRABAJO DEL
APLACADO DE PIEDRA "SANT VICENS".

PERFIL RESISTENTE,ESTRUCTURA
AUTOPORTANTE DE ALUMINIO

ANCLAJES DE FE
GALVANIZADO

PANEL BETONYP

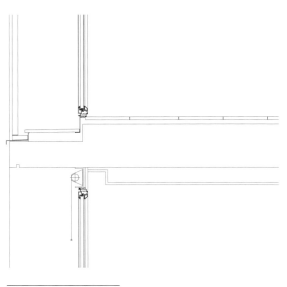

Gran Via 512

Roger de Flor 78

Rosselló 257

The brief was to convert an office building so that it might be used for apartments. The building, which dates from 1962, was by the architect Roberto Terradas Via and is considered a Property of Cultural Interest with a level of protection C in the Heritage Catalogue of Barcelona.

After the architect's children had been consulted and the need to adapt it to both current norms and the criteria of the technical code taken on board, the refurbishment of this piece of modern heritage gets underway by showing great respect towards the original scheme.

Abiding by the compositional criteria of the façade giving onto Carrer Rosselló and the façade looking out over the Palau Robert gardens, such materials as white limestone, gray granite and colored ceramic are respected, with metalwork and new steel window-frames being incorporated.

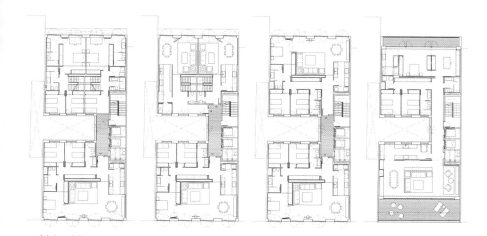

Floor plans

Passeig de Gràcia

Housing building in Passeig de Gràcia 99

Floor plans

Pg. de Gràcia 23 / Diputació 259

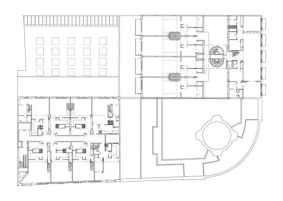

Typical floor plan

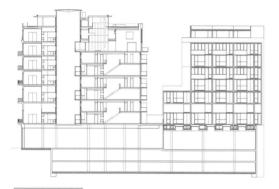

Section

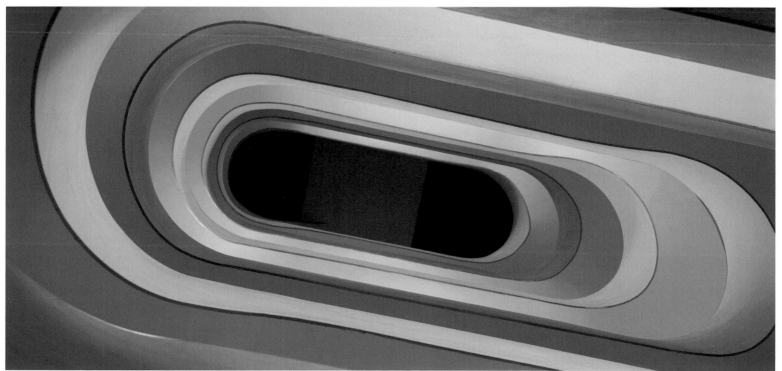

Hotel Mandarin in Pg. de Gràcia 38-40

The Mandarin Hotel situated on Paseo de Gracia in Barcelona is the result of a complex architectural exercise that resolves the implantation of a facility of international scope in a building dating from the Spanish port-war period situated in the heart of Cerdà's Ensanche.

The intervention on the old headquarters of the Banco Hispano Americano is based on thinking in urban terms in order to understand the buildings as an extension of the Paseo de Gracia that has to permit the community of the public space in its interior.

To that end, a longitudinal axis has been design that connects the building from the street until the interior of the city block. This axis is an itinerary that covers the following sequence: the Paseo de Gracia, the entrance porch situated in the main façade, whose objective is to achieve permeability towards the interior, the access ramp in an ascending sense that ends in a landing in a central position in the building, the open atrium with natural light via a glass roof light and artificial light via the geometric lines of the window frames in the corridors leading to the rooms, the landing of the mezzanine floor, which holds the hotel enclosure and from which issue all the accesses to the different facilities and, finally, the interior of the city block, holding the terrace-garden dominated by the powerful presence of the interior façade, whose intervention has consisted in providing the building's original structure with a "veil" while conserving its volumetry.

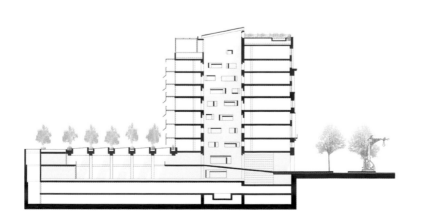

Longitudinal section

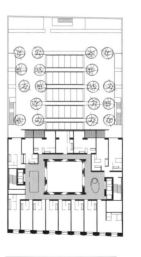

Typical floor plan

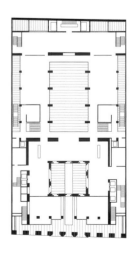

Mezzanine plan

Interior Design: Patricia Urquiola

Passeig de Gràcia 30

The new building for the Paseo de Gracia marks the search for a new forma expression. The new situation of a private building that is residential and at the same time has public spaces in Barcelona's Ensanche is understood as a continuation of the line of research undertaken over the last few years by our studio.

The organization in grids which began in the Botanical Garden project and continued in the foyer of the Hotel Juan Carlos I or in the search for three-dimensional shapes in the Benidorm Promenade, among other designs, culminates in the scheme for the Paseo de Gracia with an extremely deep facade obtained in accordance with ruled surfaces elicited by the movements of the horizontal and the vertical plane. Huge "ribs" of great slimness and varying shape construct the structural facade, creating intermediary, and at times intimate, spaces connecting inside and outside. These spaces are linked to the interior program and project outwards on occasions. This ability to generate a spatial quality on the facade is reproduced on the inside via intermediary spaces that articulate the different halls and rooms. A large patio, fashioned round two elliptical structural sections, provides light for the interior distances. In this way any other type of additional structure is done away with.

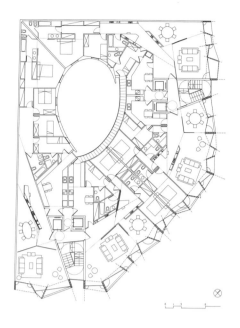

Typical floor plan

Enric Massó, mayor of Barcelona from 1973 to 1975

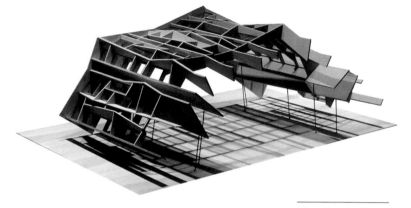

Model image

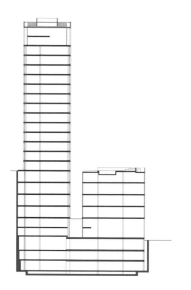

Passeig de Gràcia 109-111 – Avenida Diagonal

Cerdà intended his plan for Barcelona's Eixample to start out from a spot that would later be called the Cinc d'Oros—the Five of Diamonds—adjoining the barrio of Gràcia.

In that location Ildefons Cerdà had Avenida Diagonal intersect with Passeig de Gràcia, the two foundational and main axes of the city's expansion, and upon this schema he described the grid. Francoism eradicated the Cinc d'Oros as a location and eliminated the sculpture symbolizing the Republic. In 1957, following a competition in which some of the finest architects in Catalunya participated, Deutsche Bank chose the proposal for its bank building that has survived to this day. Hieratic and ostensibly monumental, the edifice obtained a license but remained outside current planning norms, due to which the only alternative when remodeling and adapting it to the new uses and demands of the twenty-first century would entail a remodeling which remained absolutely faithful to the volume and profile of the existing building.

Carlos Ferrater

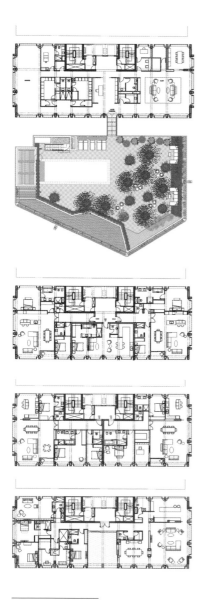

Floor plans

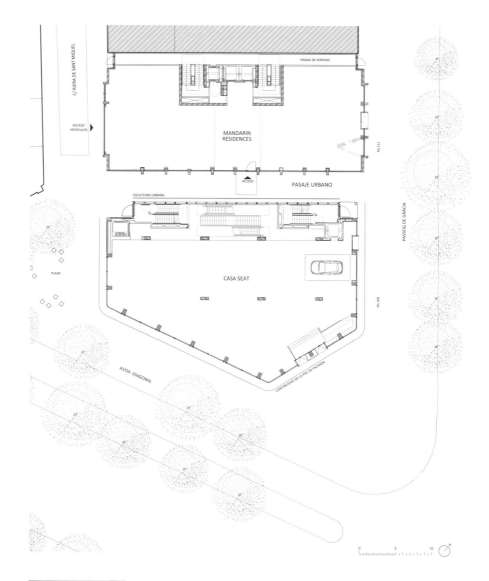

Situation plan

Its design draws on what is already there by cutting the building into two independent volumes that create a passageway which meanders between them from Passeig de Gràcia (Els Jardinets) to the half-turned Church of the Capuchins (Pompeia) on the Diagonal, forming a small square at the end of Ricra de Sant Miquel at its meeting with Avenida Diagonal.

The front volume with its bronze structural façade with large plate-glass windows and an institutional character, destined to become the new headquarters of Casa SEAT, has a split-level ground floor and five floors and intermediates with the neighboring buildings forming the frontage of Avenida Diagonal. The new stand-alone pentagonal volume eliminates its obelisk-facing curved side whilst delineating its curvilinear-shaped corners, arriving at a façade that is continuous on four of its sides, presenting its rear façade to the passageway as a blank wall, a support for a large-scale urban sculpture that will accompany movement along the passageway.

Six meters from the ground, the canopy is open to the visual cone of the passer-by whilst offering protection from the sun, especially in summer, as does the bronze serigraphy of the windows on the upper floors.

Giving frontally onto the passageway, the second volume acts as an entrance atrium to the new lobby of the residential building. The tower block displays its great slimness on the façades that are side on to Passeig de Gràcia and Avenida Diagonal, becoming ever slenderer at its extremities. It is built with a pearly steel frame that accommodates in its recesses the butting windows, which, coplanar with the frame, appear as if suspended, reflecting the city.

The sixth floor of the residential tower block is given over to add-on services for the apartments such as a social club and bar, a business center and meeting rooms or a gymnasium. From it one accedes by crossing the passageway via a lightweight bridge to the front building's garden terrace, for the exclusive use of the residences.

In doing so, the new project constructs a pedestrian passageway, an urban space which articulates a complex proposal at the same time as it differentiates the new uses and offers to the city a permeable and contemporary design in one of its most emblematic and central locations.

Views from 16th floor

View from the base of the passage at street level

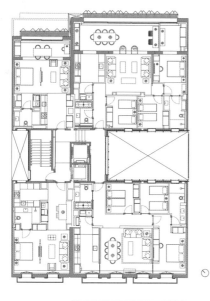

Typical floor plan

Passeig de Gràcia 125-127

The project involves the joining together and refurbishment of two party wall apartment houses in Passeig de Gràcia.

The excavation of the central bay that originally coincided with the stairways of the two houses has led to the opening of a new patio and the positioning of a new decentered staircase core and elevators, enabling access to the different levels exiting between the two properties to be resolved.

This operation has, moreover, permitted the redefining of the original typological schema of excessively deep through apartments, half of the street-side façade and small patios by new dwellings curving round the façade giving onto Carrer Riera de Sant Miquel or Passeig de Gràcia, with an interior patio façade of very generous dimensions.

The construction of the new decentered core has permitted the combining of a through store with a picture window on Passeig de Gràcia.

The intervention on the Passeig de Gràcia façade has involved a refurbishment with the maintaining of its protected features.

Originally defined as a façade with an interior gallery typical of the Eixample city block, the Riera de Sant Miquel façade has retained the proportion of the openings and its individual features of interest (pillars and cast-iron beams) and in front a new façade of lightweight movable shutters has been delaminated, facilitating protection from the setting sun and acting as a visual filter with respect to the immediate neighbors.

Xavier Martí Galí

From the <u>Royal Quarters</u> to the <u>Granada Science Park</u>

Carlos Ferrater

In Granada, a few years after building the Jardines de la Cuba del Cuarto Real next to the Arab district of Realejo, under the direction of Yolanda Brasa Quba, commissioned by the city council, we won the design competition for the extension of the Science Park in Granada, next to the river Genil. The project was conceived as the construction of a single roof with small inflections that looks like an open hand, covering the different programmatic pieces interconnected in a continuous space.

The empty space that connects the large boxes or programme containers: Macroscope, Biodome, Tecnoforum, Health Sciences, Al Andalus, auditoriums and spaces for temporary and permanent exhibitions, structures communications, logistics and relationships with the Park activities. The proposed spatial structure allows for the flexibility of uses and situations that interconnect paths and themes.

The majority of the projects developed as topographies often substitute the continuous quality of the roof with a succession of planes or different shaped porches. In this way, the space and the roof's constructive autonomy as a continuous element turns into a sequential relation of interconnected spaces.

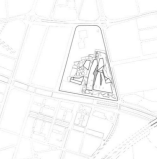

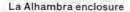

La Alhambra enclosure **Jardines del Cuarto Real** **Granada Science Park**

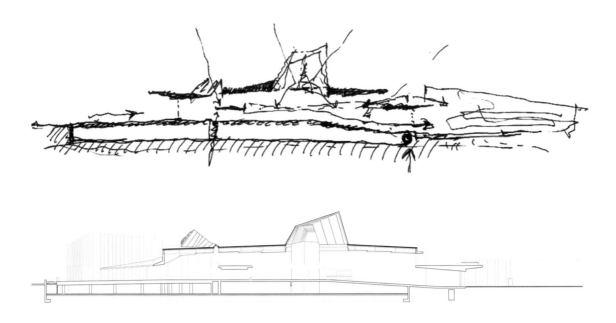

In Granada, the roof is a folded continuous surface that floats over the inclined plane of the ground level, enclosing the large exhibition spaces between them, highlighting the communication and relation spaces with the light that penetrates between the folded planes.

On its abstraction, the large roof has a profile that is similar to the skyline of the Granada Mountain range. The development of the large topographic roof adapts to the volumetric requirements that create the large, tall, enclosed spaces that house the various programmes in its interior.

The roof flies over the terrain, constructing a new topography that as it folds, organises between folds, the skylights that provide natural light to the circulation and connecting spaces.

The roof mesh is resolved with a double-layer three-dimensional structure that encloses services and technical systems, solving the rain water evacuation. The skylights guide the roof as a continuation of the main structure.

Park and City

The first steps of the Project have been based on understanding the expansion of the Science Park as an opportunity to respond to issues of urban order that transcend the Site and that contribute to shaping an area of great importance to the City.

The relationship with the River Genil and the connection with adjacent spaces of centrality have been the mainspring of the Project's urban dimension. From the start, the latter dismisses the idea of a totem building installed "above the City" and pays attention instead to the various locations of the edges and points of contact with what already exists.

These concerns have configured an organism that houses different types of space beneath a single roof, which, with slight inflections and an outer skin resembling that of a hand, enables the Park and the City to occupy the intermediary spaces -between the fingers -which accommodate the components of the programme. The footbridge linking the opposite bank of the Genil is the arm that brings the City into the Park, a new pedestrian access that connects with points of intense activity, encounter and meeting.

A new way of traversing the Park "hors control" enables us to take in the Complex from a high position and even to cross the lobby over the main Skylight, while appreciating the space and the bustle on the inside, which descending towards the access plaza, leads us to the entrance of the building and the ticket office area.

Interactivity

The idea of interactivity is present on all levels regarding the Park. Spatial continuity and intensification of the interactive potential between Building and City are the Proposal's main theme.

The Enclosure shares its public dimension with the City by means of new urban routes that are interconnected with interior circulations.

Just as the Park focuses its attention on the interactive exhibition of its themed areas, the Project provides all visitors with spaces in which to move with total freedom, accessibility and continuity. Discovering the possible routes among the many options will convert the user into an interested and inquisitive individual who takes on an active role.

Flexibility

The proposed spatial structure allows for total flexibility of use and for diverse configurations interweaving routes and themed areas. This entails converting the experience of the space into an area for games and fun. Intersecting glances, a rapport with the landscape and confined spaces are revealed throughout the visit.

Spatial organisation

The idea of an "enigmatic box" awakens the curiosity and subtly displays its interior as an invitation to be discovered in prolongation with the space of the street.

A single undulating plane floats ten metres high and is sustained by the structure of the programme's huge main boxes, defining in its interstices the vast space of the lobby, a permanent reference for both interior and exterior routes, underlined by the low-angled light of the façade windows and emphasised in the heart of the building by the great glazed fissure identifying the Park on a Metropolitan scale.

The main function of this lobby will be to lead and direct the visitor within the Complex; it receives the flow of people from the access plaza and the Green space next to the River and sends them to the extended open spaces already inside the enclosure: the Nature Plaza or Biodome and the Observatory Plaza.

Suitable programmatic features intensify the porosity surrounding the Complex: mini-cinemas, Internet cafés, a cyber library and shopping areas are set out in continuity with the platform of the public Green Space constituted in the Vestibule of the Cultural Gallery, from where people can also move onto the Macroscopio and the rest of the park. Accessibility is a basic premise of the entire circulation system.

Given its clear identity within the Complex, the Al-Andalus Science Pavilion helps maximise the interactive aspect between the City and the Park. Its entrances are independent and include a public green space nearby. Light is the main rationale for organising the spaces. Four skylights over four courtyards determine the interior, configuring a flexible base for the organisation of the themed spaces.

Sustainability, recycling and collection

The new building becomes a genuine support of these contemporary statements, which are obligatory in large-scale public projects.

The choice of material fulfils technological innovation and energy-saving ecological criteria, supporting and simplifying maintenance and good conservation.

A new urban plane is configured, the large roof, as an abstraction of the furrowed textures of the Vega flatland.

Sections of the roof are adapted to harness solar energy, permitting optimal heating and cooling costs. Other sections are containers for material recycled from building work and other industrial processes: ceramic, plastic, glass, concrete and metal, which will be classified and processed in situ to become ballast and surfacing material.

Eduardo Jiménez - Yolanda Brasa

GENIL

01 Access
02 Auditorium
03 Cultural Gallery
04 Tecno-Forum Hall
05 Al-Andalus Pavilion and Science
06 Biodome

07 Temporary Exhibition Hall
08 Pavilion "Travel to the Human Body
09 Pavilion "Cultural Hall of Prevention"
10 Circulations
11 Garden Genil
12 Forest of Feelings

0   10   20   50

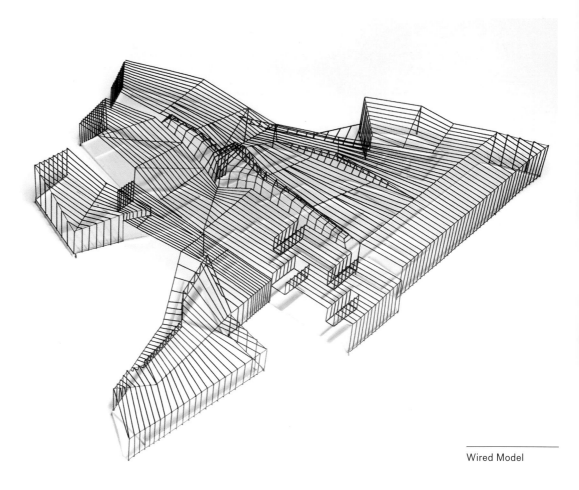

Wired Model

Ernesto Páramo Sureda

Director of Granada Science Park

Containment and moderation

If you ever see a giant termite the image will stay with you forever. This fabulous animal construction takes over our minds in a mysterious way. Its beauty is geological, mineral, powerful but restrained. Its formal design and incredible efficiency is overwhelming. Some places have that magnetic hold over us, whether it is natural or man-made. We search the world just to experience it. Ayers Rock, the large red rock in Australia or the remote Inca Machu Picchu. Many years later we still remember them with a strange closeness. What is the secret?

With the current technical means and the huge variety of resources and materials available, it is really easy to succumb to stridency and ostentation. This is why it is so great to be able to appreciate both a sober and beautiful building. A true exercise of restraint and sobriety.

I've never been interested in the whole architecture "show". Not only because it often contains a rare blend of technical prowess and banality, but above all because construction clashes with the essence of the show that in order to be so, has a limited duration. We may enjoy a show, provided it doesn't last too long. A building is too long-term for this purpose.

Today the element of surprise is overrated. So much so that more and more buildings are being built in order to surprise rather than for practical purposes and to describe them as functional is often pejorative. I mean really! No one would choose a decorative pacemaker instead of one that works. As this disastrous trend begins to subside, our commitment has been clear and the result is in sight.

In architecture, as in science and communication, we should always have the famous Occam's Razor on hand.

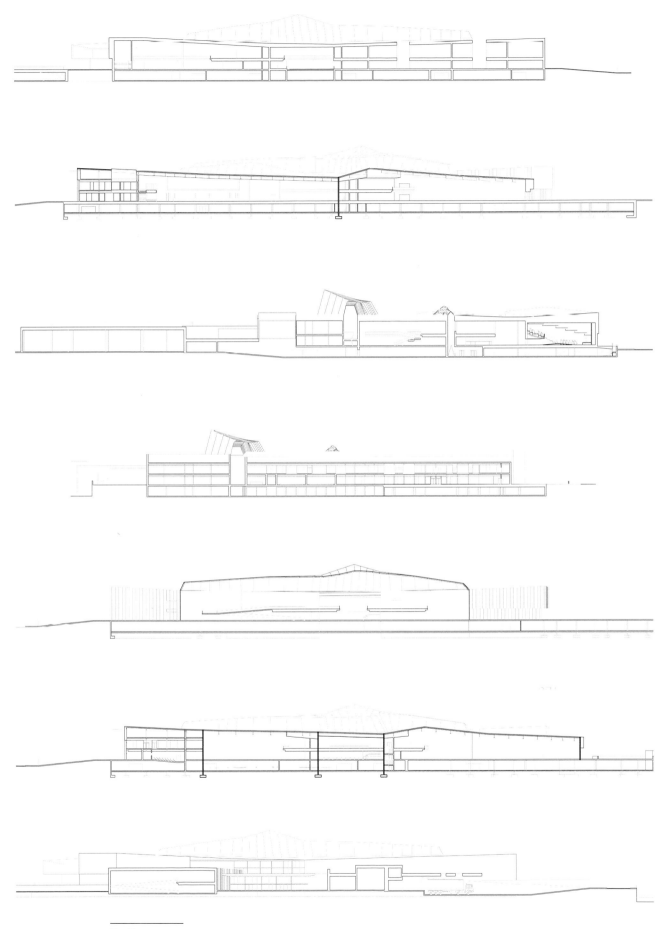

Sections

On the <u>Bilbao river side</u>

Multihousing in Bilbao

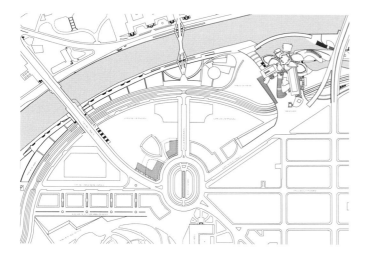

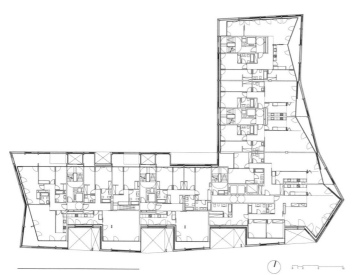

Block A. 7th Level

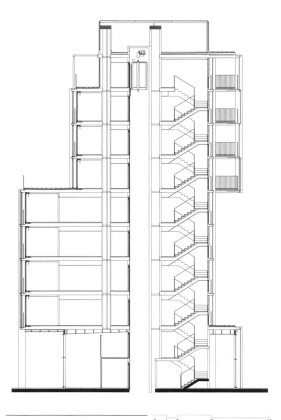

Block A. Cross Section

0 1 2   5   10

Respecting historicist criteria on the delimitation of the nineteenth century elliptical square, the project takes on a contemporary quality producing a building front in the Plaza de Euskadi. By means of individual blocks on the ground floor and the 8 floors flanking the tower, its alignment is parallel to the Duesto Bridge project, which is vested in the symbolic nature of its unique site.

The project proposes, as a resolution to the buildings, dwellings that span façade to façade, which will allow for better orientation, permit cross-ventilation, and will improve the amount of natural light.

Great typological versatility exists in the proposition of the dwellings as 1, 2, and 3 bedroom houses and 2 and 3 bedroom duplexes. The buildings will become empty from a pre-determined floor, on, providing the buildings with spaces for private or semi-private use, and creating visuals and drawing diverse and differentiated sky-lines towards Plaza Euskadi or the Campa de los Ingleses.

The volume is defined by the treatment of the outer casing, patterned after structural ribs that span the height of the structure, covered by a sulfurized brass that bring the access gate to the floor. The thermal controls have coated modules in order to control the solar radiation and heat loss, and are produced by the treatment and finishing of skins.

IMQ Hospital in Bilbao

A building of a unitary, global kind that constructs a landscape, given that it has interiorized Bilbao's genetic code, determined by the modernity of a highly contemporary geometry and the industrial tradition of the city.

The project defines an envelope that binds together the different parts of this complex hospital program in the podium. Said program is defined by the abstract treatment of the outer skin, punctuated by structural ribs extending vertically up the entire height of the building. The flexible modulation allows for great versatility when it comes to subdividing the interior space.

The polygonal facade converts the hospitalization block into the icon of the building, responding to the location by becoming the gateway of the future remodeling of Zorrozaurre and configuring a new urban frontage on the estuary, in keeping with the Guggenheim and the Euskalduna Palace.

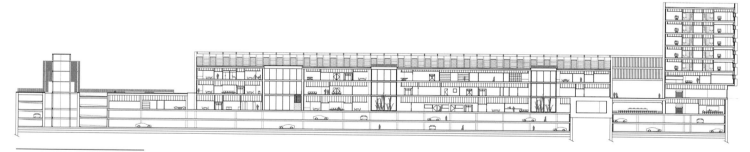

Longitudinal Section

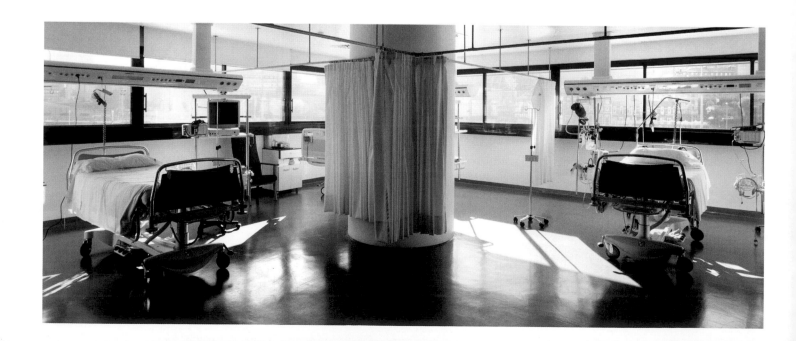

Between the sea and the Venetian Lagoon

Carlos Ferrater

The Italian experience

After graduating in the early 70's from the Barcelona school of architecture, virtually paralysed by the political situation of the late Franco regime, trips to northern Italy were a breath of fresh air because there the world of architecture and design led by Gardela, Albini, Peresutti and Rogers, Ponti, Gregotti or Magistretti but also by designers like Sotsass, Colombo, Mendini or Zanusso, seemed to recognise or renew the legacy of the avant-garde rationalists of the 30s following suit from the generation of Terragni, Moretti, Figini and Pollini, Ridolfi and Libera.

New Italian architecture genealogically reconstructed the line of succession while in the school of Venice, Tafuri, Escolari, Aymonino and Rossi formulated the theoretical bases of a new theory of the city, which in a few years would result in dogma blocking the future production of Italian architecture. By breaking the continuity of modern tradition that paradoxically re-emerged in Catalan architecture through the teachings brought to Catalonia by the creators of the School of Barcelona.

The exhibition at the Triennale di Milano by José Antonio Coderch de Sentmenat and in particular the mediation by Oriol Bohigas, Federico Correa and Ignasi de Solà-Morales and a group of young teachers from the school of architecture in Barcelona set the stage and planted the seed that in the 80s and early 90s marked the emergence of Catalan architecture and especially the urban transformation of Barcelona.

My memories of trips to northern Italy in the 70s, preferably Milan and Venice, represent a time of learning, knowledge and familiarity of their cultural and historical models.

In recent years, Italy and in particular the city of Venice has been the most frequent destination of my visits, panels, project corrections and conferences sponsored by Professor Eleonora Mantese in the Venice Institute of Architecture. In the early years, still in the campus of San Polo, she showed us an off-the-beaten track Venice and thus a friendship formed that led us to collaborate in the competition for the extension of "Cimitero de la isola de San Michele". We competed alongside David Chipperfield and Enric Miralles. I remember an extraordinary boat ride along the Venetian Lagoon along with Benedetta Tagliabue in which we were shown the old cemetery, its secrets and problems such as the slow mineralisation of the bodies due to the humidity and pollution of the sludge drained from the Venetian canals used in its construction.

Design competition for the Isola di San Michele cemetery

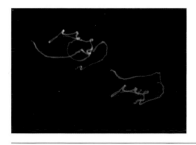

Kites flying in the night skies over Venice   Workshop in Venice with Eleonora Mantese

Years later, in the new Cottonifficcio school, we developed a project workshop in the summer of 2004 with Eleonora Mantese, Christiana Eusepi and Gustavo Carabajal and I remember the exciting night flight of the "aquilones" constructed by students on the canals of Venice. After the academic collaboration, I asked Eleonora and Gustavo to collaborate on the project, sponsored by the Veneto planning consultant, Danilo Gerotto, a private Venetian developer who had the idea to carry out the project from a public-private agreement on the Lido di Jesolo, which consisted of the renovation of public space in the centre of the town and construction of facilities and services that would frame the Aquileia Tower, standing 100 metres high, it would be by far the tallest tower on the Venetian landscape.

Located between the mouth of the River Sile and Piave, between the sea and the lagoon, the project built in part through the efforts and dedication of Gustavo Carabajal, its profile has become the new emblem of the town.

In recent years, after being awarded a Doctor Honoris Causa from the University of Trieste in February 2006, our new studio has been invited to participate in several competitions in various locations in Italy. As a result of this period, we are currently working with Domenico Piemonte on projects such as the remodelling of Castello Borelli and its hydraulic devices in which we proposed the creation of a small residential settlement in the form of a plaza suspended over the sea in a fissure in Monte Piccaro between the towns of Borghetto and Cerialli in the region of Liguria. This project, together with our recent work has been exhibited at the invitation of Ordine degli Architetti di Roma in the magnificent Roman Aquarium in Rione Monti, throughout September, an exhibition curated by Paolo Maselli, one of our studio's partners.

Project for the remodelling of Castello Borelli, Liguria

Throughout the 2009-2010 academic year, together with Alberto Peñín and with the collaboration of Stella Rahola and Jordi Vidal, we have developed proposals for the new port in Venice next to the church of Santa Elena, in the context of the Projects XXI Master's Degree which we teach for the Fundació UPC in the OAB gallery and in the School of Architecture of Barcelona.

For us, Italy has been and will be in the coming years, our favourite destination for our work, both for its cultural proximity and affinity with many young architects who have been carrying out their apprenticeship in our studio, and for their renewed interest in the contemporary project.

"Projects XXI" Master's Degree. Scale Model of Venice in clay

Gustavo Carabajal

The project falls between the Venice lagoon, the mouth of the Rivers Sile and Piave and the sea, and is integrated through an axis perpendicular to the coastline and extends from the Piazza Internazionale, Via Aleardi, Piazza Mazzini, Via Bafile and the beach, penetrating the sea by four hundred metres. The penetration system is an alternative to the traditional longitudinal system typical of this area.

An underground public car park in Piazza Internazionale with a tree-lined path that alternates between sun and shade, the remodelling of Via Aleardi with the formation of a new public space, the two thousand square metre Piazza Aquileia, surrounded by a two-level building that contains various commercial uses and facilities such as shops, cafes, restaurants and fitness and a sun terrace and pool. A passage serves as the entrance to the underground parking and the logistics of the tower and shopping complex. In the middle of this space surrounded by these buildings stands the Aquileia tower one hundred metres high.

The project includes the regeneration of the Piazza Mazzini, at the junction of Via Aleardi and Bafile, as a space that organises the intervention. The plaza is thought of as a changing space that supports various uses. This place, paved in stone with trees and lighting, a large bench and a set of sprinklers, sprays and fountains, allows for a multitude of uses and control of the road traffic as well as multiple environmental possibilities. On the south side of the plaza, a large window to the sea, shaped by residential buildings and a quay in the form of a Promenade that penetrates the sea and creates a small dock for the occasional mooring of small boats, completes the intervention.

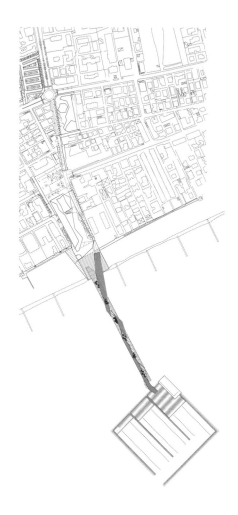

Intervention plan

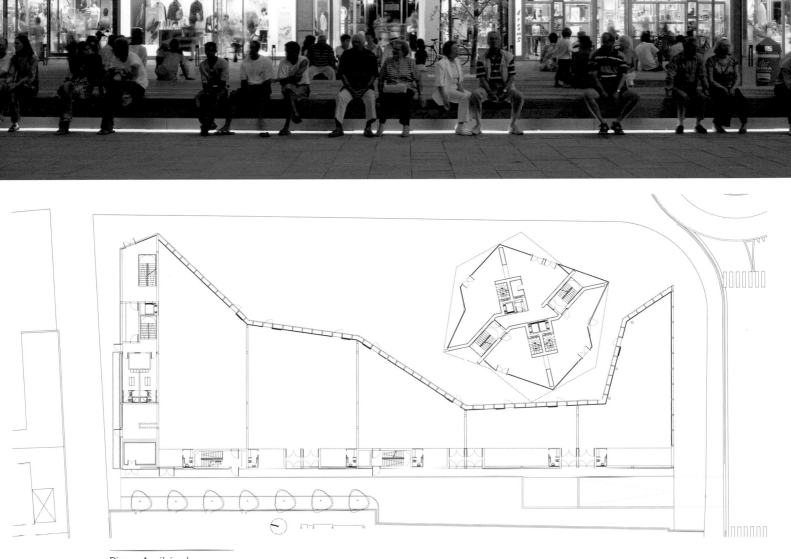

Piazza Aquileia plan

The 24 storey Aquileia tower is structured with a double height ground floor housing the lobby, banks and a cafeteria, two floors for offices and 22 floors with different residential apartments. The polygonal profile organised around the vertical circulation cores, lifts and emergency staircases, provides the four apartments on each floor, of which two are one bedroom and two are two bedrooms,, with views from the terraces of both the sea and lagoon. The houses facing west have views of the campaniles (bell towers) and the city centre of the city of Venice, while the apartments facing east offer views of the rivers and the distant horizon of the Dolomites.

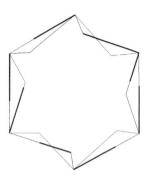
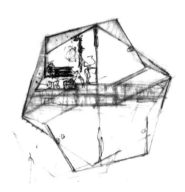
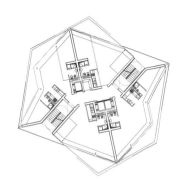

This configuration means that privacy is maintained while allowing for the construction of the intermediate i.e. interior-exterior spaces. These polygonal shaped terraces become living spaces; an extension of the home, their use is made more flexible through sliding glass walls and blinds, becoming a real environmental and climate filter, adjusting the light and shade, and views. The ensemble of the façades is a lightweight, subtle and versatile material that dematerialises the skin, while maintaining the tectonic image of the tower.

The building is crowned with two outstretched sail-shaped pinnacles, which when lit up at night become a night-time landmark from afar. They act as structural brackets attached to the concrete nucleus, supported through tensors that force the projections of the façades perimeter to work by traction.

On the ground floor, large glass expanses hide the structure and help to balance the volume of the tower with the stony surface of the plaza.

The apartments of sixty and seventy-five square metres with terraces between twenty and thirty square metres consist of an access programme, living room, dining room, kitchen and one or two bedrooms with their respective bathrooms.

In summary, the Aquileia tower project, as an iconic piece throughout Veneto, offers a recognisable profile in an area of low-rise building, playing with the fog and the light of the Adriatic area and becomes the main argument of a new urban system focusing on centrality.

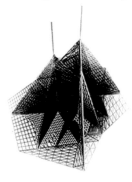

Building Social Utopia

El Prat, Baix Llobregat

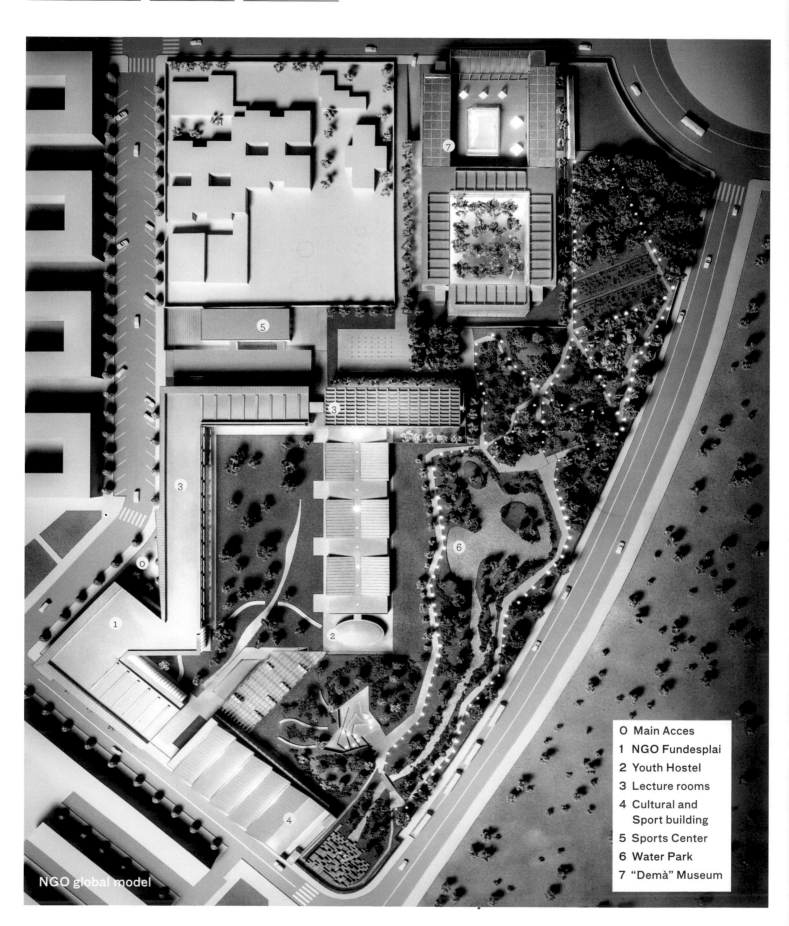

NGO global model

0 Main Acces
1 NGO Fundesplai
2 Youth Hostel
3 Lecture rooms
4 Cultural and
   Sport building
5 Sports Center
6 Water Park
7 "Demà" Museum

NGO Centre Esplai

The project for the Fundació Esplai and its location in the troubled San Cosme district in Baix Llobregat began with the construction of its administrative headquarters, a first hostel, a sports hall and some spaces for training.

The foundation is intended to offer social inclusion and environmental conservation, all with a clear desire for sustainability.

Its tremendous social work focuses on families in situations of marginalisation, and particularly the children of these families, offering them the chance to stay in holiday centres in natural settings all over Catalonia. It also builds hostels and nature education centres and provides soup kitchens and catering for schools.

The building of additional facilities alongside its main headquarters has now begun. They include sports halls and multi-use rooms, an extension of the initial hostel to 450 people, a large training room, a forum for debates and a planned "Museum of Tomorrow", which will deal with the area of "sustainable nutrition, the fight against climate change, social inclusion and, above all, phenomena that disrupt the future of our society".

NGO Lecture rooms

Among these new facilities, we present the new classroom and the space for meetings and debates, which have now been completed. An elliptical agora, like the one drawn by Hypatia of Alexandria, in the 5th century, as a geometric space in which the sum of the distances from each point to the foci always remains constant. That is the starting point for a place for training and debate.

The classroom is related to the other buildings in the complex, forming a Mediterranean cloister garden, flanked by a water park that will show the route of the water of the Baix Llobregat to the sea. This will complement the initial facilities – a site intended to serve people, and especially children.

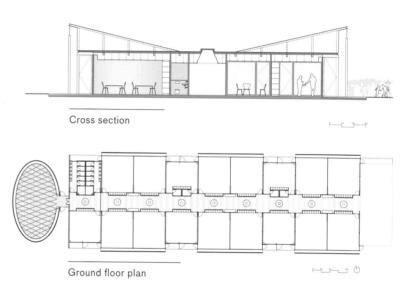

Cross section

Ground floor plan

"The summers of childhood are the homeland where dreams reside".

—Josep Gassó - Fundesplai President

Viladoms - Montserrat Chidren's Summer camp

Breaking off from the conventional types of holiday homes which only follow the "comb scheme", we propose to create individual units that will all relate to each other, but still remain autonomous units. The ratio of floor area increases, and communication between the units is possible through outer walkways.

Volumetric fragmentation allows small autonomous units to graduate the number of users and minimize the costs of maintenance and supervision, while allowing configuration of a system within the whole colony.

The unit is proposed as a benchmark archetype and image of the imaginary world of childhood: small houses, small people, relationship with the forest, roads, and nature that allow for easy extension and expansion of the system itself.

We propose 3 different room types, with groups of 4, 6 or 8 children, with the opportunity to develop a level or two as the body, resulting in the end of a total capacity of 90 places. The upper space and volume of air has acquired great importance given that the ambience of the rooms favors the incorporation of acoustic control and artificial illumination provided by white, tube lighting suspended from the ceiling.

The simplicity of the materials used has allowed greater economic viability by means of implementation, final impact, and subsequent maintenance.

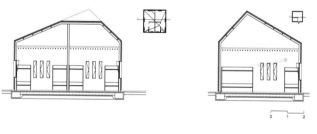

The location of the sets of vertical windows allows perfect cross ventilation, regardless of the prevailing wind in each case.

For the exterior, the uniqueness in the materials of the façades and roofs, both in the cellular rooms public buildings, a flexible and self-cleaning stucco that allows for continuity and insulation around the water-repellent treated perimeter.

The final proposed solution allows for a broad spectrum of users; not just schoolchildren summer campers, but also families and groups who will want to use the camp facilities year round.

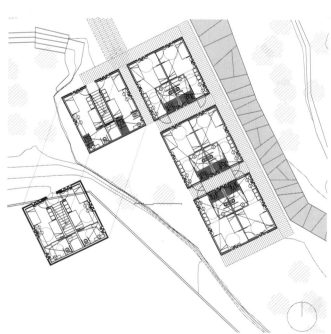

La Rectoria Children's Summer camp in Solsona

The Rectoría de la Selva hostel is located where the rectory of the church of Sant Climent once stood. The current church was built during the 17th century and, like the belfry, is made of squared and textured stone. The church is south-facing, with a rectangular apse to the north. Not all was newly built, for part of the front wall and the lower stretches of the belfry might have made use of the earlier Romanesque church. On the main façade there is a great portal with a semicircular arch and large voussoirs, plus a small rose window of stones of a certain size.

The inside of the church is simple, in the classical style, while the liturgical features are contemporary, since the original altars were destroyed during the civil war. Above the church vault there is a chamber, built at the same time as the church and the rectory. The rectory, an annex on the west wing of the church, is square in plan and has two floors. It is a building typical of El Solsonès, with a stone structure, thick walls and a gabled roof with a lining of wood.

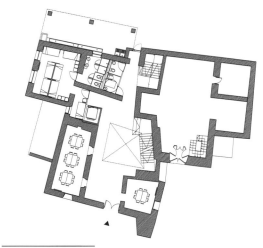

Ground floor

Second floor

Sustainable buildings

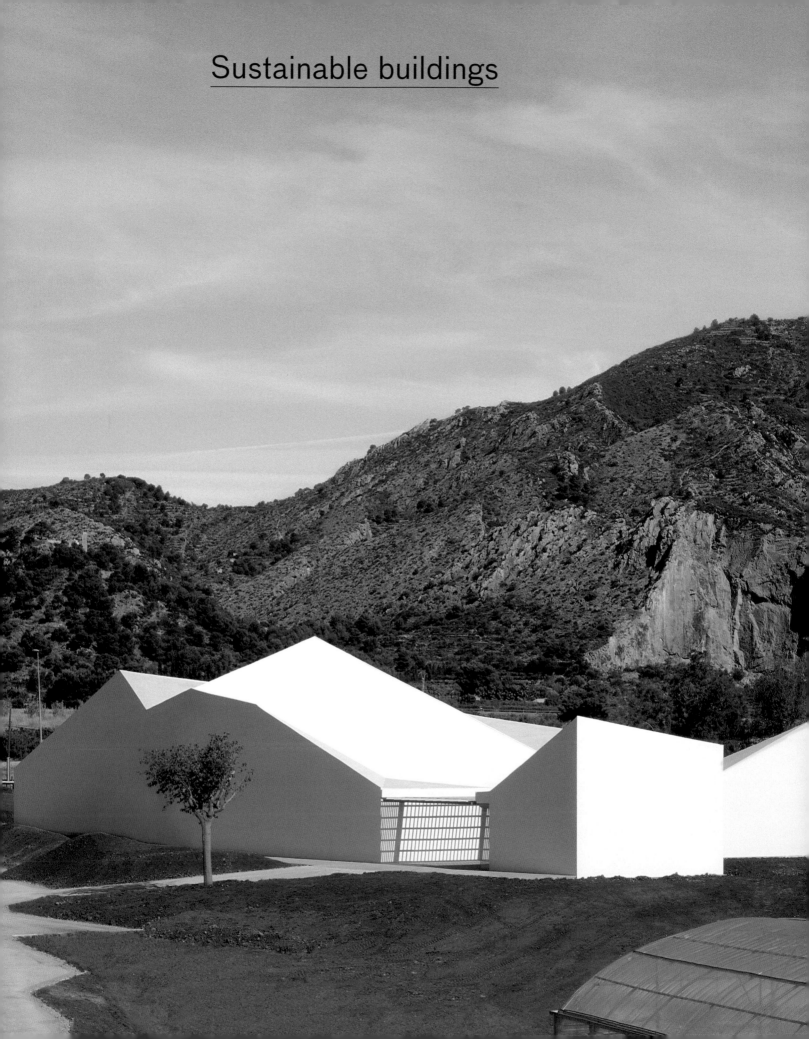

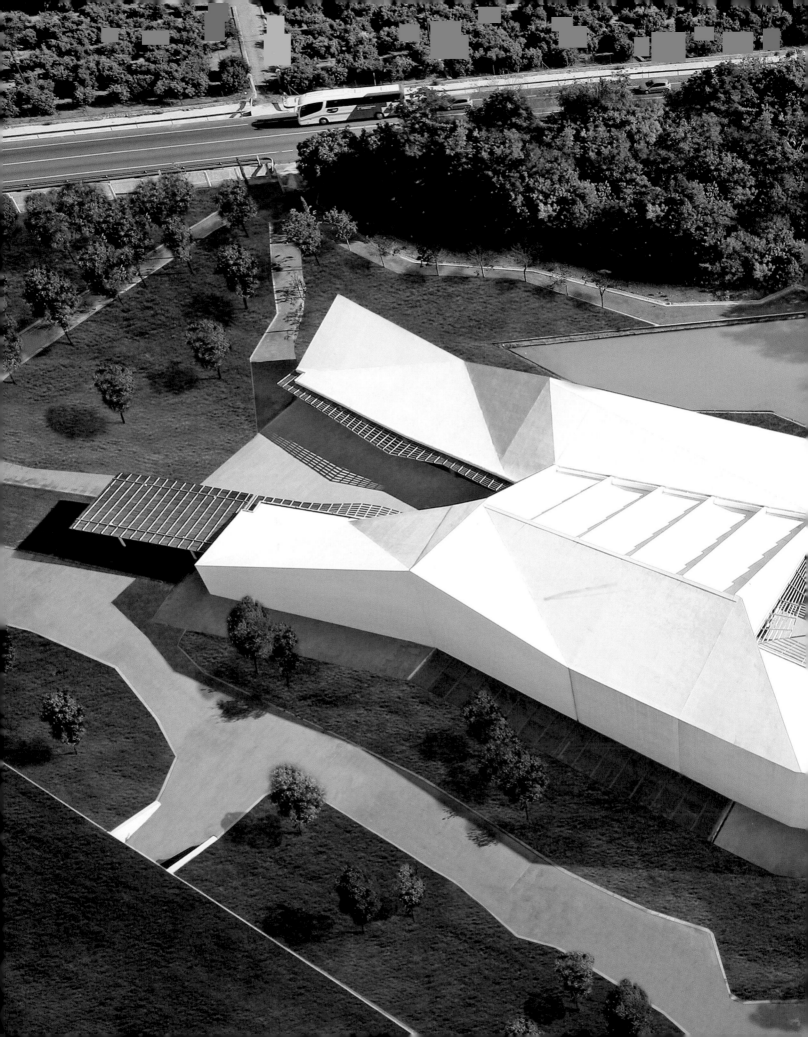

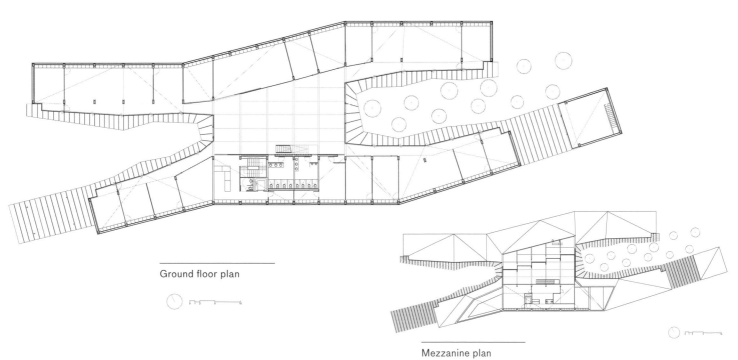

Ground floor plan

Mezzanine plan

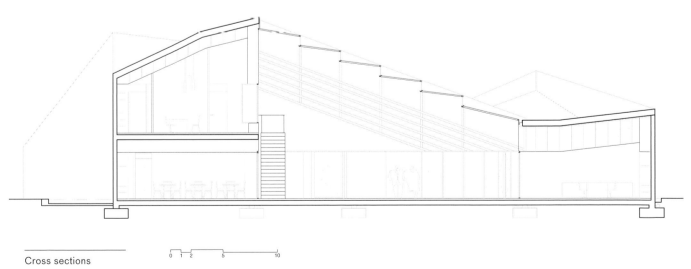

Cross sections

Grupo Azahar is a group of companies with a strong connection to sustainability and the environment. The parent company is based in Castellón. Given its growth and expansion, it required a head office that reflected its commitment to the environment and the arts, and a programme that incorporated two more actions: greenhouses and exterior plant nursery, and a complementary services building. With this framework, the owners of the Grupo Azahar invited prestigious European architectural practices to design their new headquarters, with the decision in favour of the design created by OAB.

The new building had to be autonomous with respect to the surroundings. This was a way of preserving the integrity of the landscaping on the site. A vast empty triangle without scale, the site is overshadowed by the image of the Maestrazgo Mountains and its proximity to the N-340 highway. Disconnected from the urban fabric and distant from the conditioning factors of conventional legibility, and given the proposed abstraction and geometry of the design, the strategy was for architecture to cross the bounds imposed by discipline to dissolve into the landscape.

The headquarters building has settled into the site, bringing to light the quality of what was already there, camouflaging itself with the setting. To the north and west, the mountainous topography is a backdrop for the building, against which the roof is geometrically cut away. From a distance, its faceted form and profile help to situate it in the landscape. Its tectonic design and image allow it to be described as a sculptural composition, an abstract organisation of solids and voids. The abstraction is the result of the material continuity of the surface and its opaque nature, hiding its supporting structure and the space it envelops.

The planned site layout allows the building to be shown to its best advantage, allowing the perimeter to be traversed entirely and the building to be observed from many different perspectives. Its geometry creates different views, consequence of the interplay of variable light and shade produced over the white folds of the building.

Built on an east-west axis, the building is distributed into two wings joined by a central volume and placed around two open courtyards, each with a different style. The first of these serves as an exterior foyer for receiving visitors and employees; the second is landscaped and has a more private use. Thus, the building is closed off from the distant landscape and establishes a complex interior/exterior relation.

True to the Khanian concept of "Silence and Light", the glass walls facing the courtyards allow the varying tones of natural daylight into the building's interior; they introduce the outside world directly into the interior through these intermediate spaces. Uniform silver daylight bathes the surfaces of the vaults, homogenising the lighting levels inside the building.

The courtyards allow a cross view between the wings through glass walls, with the canopy and the building's orientation helping to keep direct radiation from the inhabitable interior spaces, but allowing in a great deal of controlled light, making artificial lighting practically unnecessary.

The four wings housing different departments of the company converge on a foyer which, besides acting as a distributor, becomes a large representative exhibition space. Once entering through the main doors, not only is the palette of materials changed, but also the criteria behind their handling. While the exterior is predominantly a solid, matt and opaque image, the interior was designed with an eye for the conventions of comfort and recognition. The use of natural materials – stone and wood – offer a counterpoint to the solid abstraction of the exterior.

This foyer receives its light from above; light coming from the north enters the building through a grand skylight above a series of suspended concrete girders, paying tribute to the architects' demolished work; Restaurante Lola.

The ceilings inside reinforce the geometry of the roof and the spatial continuity by means of transparent glass tympani supported on the partitions between the different rooms.

For exterior walls a continuous cladding was chosen that could be applied seamlessly to both façades and roof blurring the lines between them. Collaboration with the R&D department of Parex gave rise to a new material applied to the Coteterm system, with continuity of the thermal insulation the length of the building's perimeter. We intended to achieve maximum energy savings and to find an environmentally-sustainable solution.

The resulting skin is of white flexible and self-cleaning stucco that does not require joints, except for those made during the actual construction measuring 2-3 mm. Special mention should be made of an important aspect – the high energy efficiency we were able to see for ourselves in the interior, given that during the summer months there is no need for supplementary air conditioning.

One important environmental aspect of the buildings is the rainwater collection from all of the roof areas and the exterior areas into a cistern-pond, for use in watering the gardens and the plant nurseries on the site.

This project won a prize during the 7th Ibero-American Architecture and Town Planning Biennial in April 2010.

Carlos Ferrater

House family of an artist in Gaüses
Sustanability house

The house is on a long, narrow site between neighbouring plots which descends from the eastern end of the main street in Gaüses to a torrent running along its western boundary. The project lay-out, determined by the topographical orientation and concern for privacy, is a set of 12.5 x 5 metre pavilions interspersed with voids or courtyards. The programme is organised in the pavilions, and the voids provide access and allow cross-ventilation and light into the interiors.

It is a simple building, efficient thanks to its insulation, which expresses the form of its construction in the materiality of its finishes. Inclined ceilings built with concrete and steel semi-beams, ceramic tongue and groove that receives the insulation, and Arab roof tiles as a finish imposed by the regulations are complemented with walls of white stuccoed blocks and polished concrete floors.

Outside, there is a garden with native species as an extension of the local landscape, a small swimming pool and a movable pergola designed by Pete Sans.

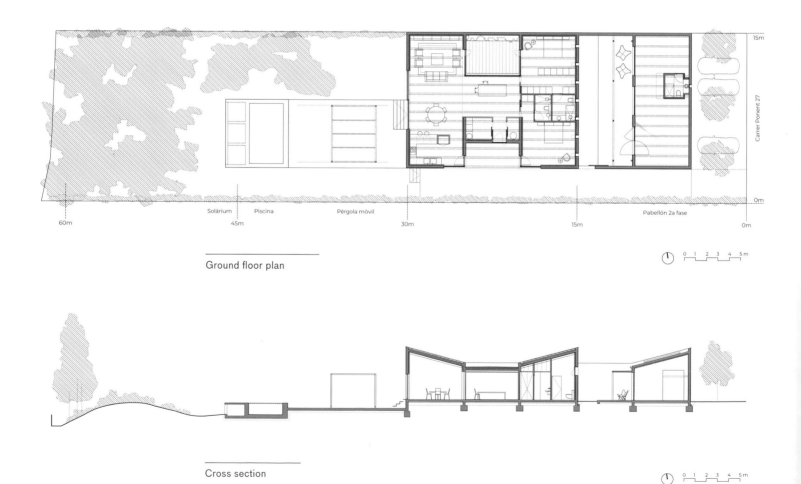

Ground floor plan

Cross section

Photo by Carlos Ferrater

Urban actions

Alenti Hotel

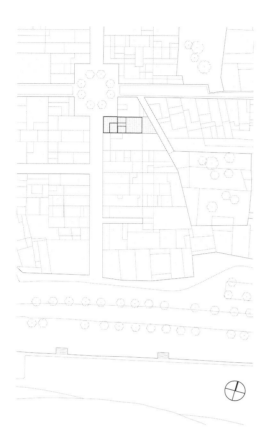

Ground floor plan

Typical floor plan

restaurante
hotel

Hotel Alenti, Sitges

Lucía Ferrater

Two projects offered us a strict programme defined by the end users and, particularly, the desire to have a representative and singular building in their urban setting.

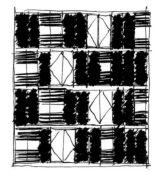

The first, a 9-room hotel, is located on the corner of a central square in Sitges, which responds to a layout of narrow and irregular streets lined with low buildings. The location is the famous Carrer 2 de Maig or "Sin Street", so-called because of its night life. The client was a developer and friend, and his young and enterprising daughter who had recently returned from the US and who, after a number of years spent on cruise ships, decided to settle down and take on the family business. The need arose to construct a contemporary building that took into account the Mediterranean tradition and the concepts of the local venacular architecture. The building is an attempt to dignify a public space by enhancing the value of the corner using a sculptural composition of gaps and voids, reflective surfaces and transparency.

The second is a Protestant church for the United Evangelical Church of Terrassa, an institution with almost one hundred years of history in the city. This community, one of the largest of its kind in Catalonia, had been struggling to find a site for a building that would combine religious and social uses. It needed to house an auditorium and a library for the Protestant Archive of Catalonia, in addition to classrooms, music rooms, a multi-purpose space and a childcare centre to serve the district.

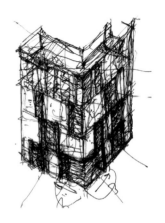

The project took several months to design, during which close contact was maintained with the community, at times with long and large meetings in the office and at others exhibiting the project in churches with 300 people. The new complex was paid for with the sale of the old building, with contributions from members of the community and with a part granted by the government in return for the commitment to a social project they would carry out.

The desire to have an austere but friendly building, without becoming an icon but at the same time unique and a reference point from the distance led us to design a single-storey project without architectural barriers.

The height of the building was reduced owing to the slope of the side streets and two cube-shaped volumes were suspended over it, which became representative owing to their size and their skin design. This new complex is located in an area between the peripheral residentail districts and the industrial area where the plots are larger and the streets are wider. It was opened by the former US president and Nobel Peace Prize winner Jimmy Carter.

This church is the last of this overview of different situations we have found in urban centres, where small actions ranging from projects in low-density residential areas to public spaces with diverse programmes have offered us the opportunity to experiment with design approaches involving the economising of means, environmental efficiency, social organisation and respect for the built-up environment and for the city.

Evangelical Church in Terrassa

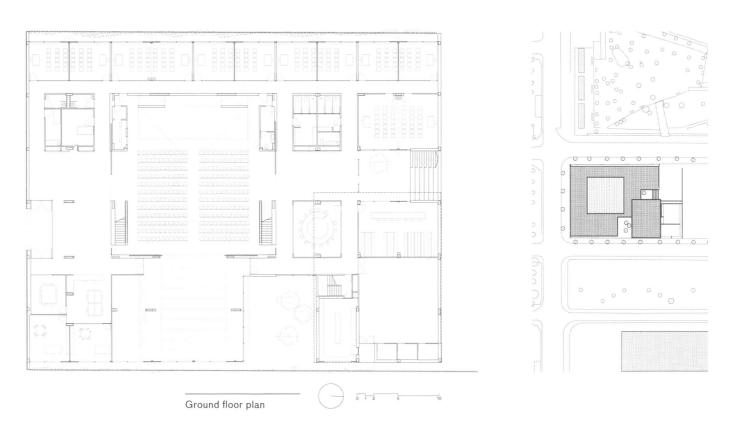

Ground floor plan

0 1 2   5   10

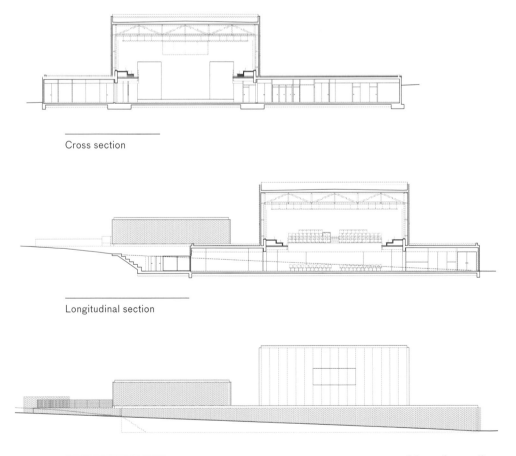

Cross section

Longitudinal section

West elevation

0 1   5   10

The United Evangelical Church of Terrassa, Barcelona finds its place in the district of Can Tusell that faces Bejar Avenue.

The building combines religious use and social use under an agreement with the city.

The complex manifests itself as a large base with two volumes suspended above it, formed by steel plates that cover the façade on one side and become a fence on the other two sides, with decreasing height due to the slope of the plot.

In the central position of the building rises a large cube with well-defined edges, which houses the sanctuary and iscovered in a new material of recycled aluminum scrapsthat gives a symbolic character to the geometric shape through its illuminative property. The other, shorter cube next to Tramuntana Street is suspended and cantilevered out. In this case, the defined edges mark the planes of perforated, corrugated aluminum lattice that acts as a second skin for the child-care program.

Renovation of the former tugboat building as the
new institutional headquarters of the Barcelona
World Race in the port of Barcelona

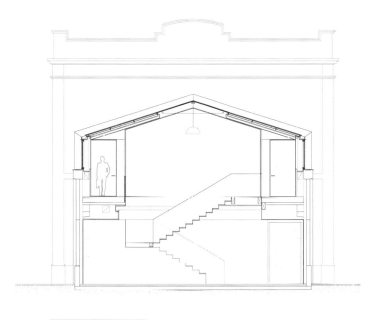

Cross section

The tugboat building, a master-built construction, dates from the beginning of the 20th century. Since then it has suffered a series of alterations of mediocre quality. Given, moreover, that it is situated at the end of a row of buildings with the same colonial port look to them, the remodeling project posits the reconstruction of its central section—the most degraded structure—the repairing of the side towers, and solely proposes a new roof that, keeping to the maximum height, includes a huge skylight in its upper crown and big picture windows on either side of the walkway and the port. The two-story building houses a shop, exhibition space and toilets within the ground floor, while on the top floor there is an office, storeroom, function room and large multiuse hall for institutional meetings.

Paris, Tolouse and Lyon

**Michelin Headquarters
Boulogne-Billancourt. Paris**

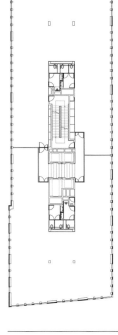

Longitudinal section

Typical floor plan

Alberto Peñin Llobell

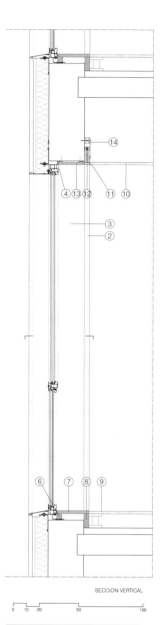

SECCION VERTICAL

0 10 20   50   100

Wall. Vertical section

1 Bottom Panel lacquered wood.
   Hidden fixations. 245x24mm
2 Top lacquered wood boards.
   Fixed on board. 40x28mm
3 Panel lacquered wood. Hidden fixations,
   205x16mm
4 Fixing galvanized steel.
5 Base board of lacquered wood. 20x24mm
   on wooden stick 110x40mm
6 Wooden stick 40x50mm
7 Support on lacquered wood.
   Hidden fixations. 205x16mm
8 Wooden stick 110x40mm
9 False ground on plots
10 Removable false ceiling
11 Continuous steel side profile,
   lacquered in white. 20x75mm
12 Stor with adjustable horizontal slats.
   Metallic silver. Crank
13 Top panel lacquered wood. 205x19mm.
   Hidden fixations. 205x19mm
14 Fixation of continuous steel side profile
   over the false ceiling.

The attention to the city postulated here is once again the initial argument behind the Boulogne building. Located on a bend in the Seine facing the Meudon Hills and with the Île Séguin as a river port, the former Renault factory site has been designated a regeneration area (Zone de Aménagement Concerté), managed by SAEM Boulogne Billancourt. This gradual redevelopment process will result in a new district that combines density, multiple uses, a restricted variety of building types and the constant presence of the river landscape. It combines different owners and developers together in an operation overseen by the public authorities by means of design competitions for every large-scale development block, architects such as Perrault – precisely with other offices, Nouvel, Foster, Diener&Diener, FOA, Mateo, Barani and Baumschlager-Eberle are involved in the design. The first project designed and built by OAB in France, coordinated by the Belgian architect Stéphane Beel, was the result of one of these competitions.

Located in the avenue leading to Île Séguin, the project reformulates the construction density of the master plan to improve its relationship with the river to the south and to the north with the city of Paris and with the commercial thoroughfare that will connect to the existing densely-populated residential area. Faced with the diversity of the plan in terms of urban development and constructions, the project proposes a classic and restrained modernity, in keeping with the town hall of Boulogne Billancourt, one of the last projects by Garnier (1934) or even with the Institute Français building (1975) by Coderch in Barcelona, in a sort of return trip. Abstraction and timelessness exuded by the building contributes to its integration in the urban setting and is the architects' strategy of working in a responsible and dedicated manner abroad.

The choice of a silvery phyllite stone module measuring 45 x 90 x 3 cm came from the effectiveness on the floor plan of having a row of 1.35-m offices. These modules were submultiples of the 90 x 270-cm window, deeply inset with a 1-cm wide extruded aluminium perimeter frame. The communications core, services, plant and structural frame are laid out along a longitudinal axis, freeing a surface area of 18 x 54.5 m. The façade was built in France in concrete and houses and optimises the rest of the structure. The stone and window modules clad this perimeter over a variable pentagram base, with slight variations and seemingly random gaps which, in some cases such as the cantilever, obey a structural logic.

Subtle changes appear at the top (ninth floor), where the modules are of a greater height and there are brise-soleil; on the corner of the Avenue Île Séguin, where the windows are set at an angle; and on the ground floor, where the vertical proportion of the void is emphasised and the commercial premises are set back for greater protection and depth. The 5.50-m cantilever next to the residential building by Stéphane Beel offers continuity to the landscaped axis that crosses all the blocks enhancing the lively commercial activity desired by the local authorities.

Four canopies are integrated into the building's exterior design to mark the entrance between stainless steel frames. They consist of a horizontal plane suspended by cables, compressing space like an antechamber to the dual-aspect foyer that opens onto the landscaped slope at the heart of the block. The interior design is completed with silvery stone facing on the lifts, matt stainless steel on their frames and joinery, American oak panelling and front desk and the integrated indirect lighting.

The façade becomes an urban texture continuing onto the street, and establishes numerous associations with the Parisian sky and rain, with its material being alive and ambivalent, dark or silvery in line with the weather and light in the city. The quality of the stone, the random lights from offices at night and reflections off the steel canopies and anodised aluminium frames contribute to dematerialise this petrous architecture.

In later years, we had the opportunity to execute two neighbourhoods in Toulouse and the Lawyers Union Headquarters in Lyon.

ZAC Monges, Tolouse

The land lot is located in one corner of the Monges ZAC development zone in the community of Cornebarrieu, pertaining to the metropolitan area of Toulouse. It involves an innovative urban experiment that posits a new kind of life in contact with nature without, for all that, forgoing a certain density in the various interventions.

The land lot is the last in a series of lots connected by an unidirectional parkway that feeds the different condominiums of the ZAC.

The project proposes a radical geometrical carpet that refers to the layout of the farmland in the region, consisting of tilled land in systematic small plots. blurred.

The intermediate areas thus generated construct a communitarian space that is able to relate to the landscape by dint of its interstitial porosity.

ZAC Andromède, Tolouse

The simplicity of the volumes proposed and their implantation corresponds to variable, dynamic typologies and reinforces city block 56's sense of being both a starting and end point. The overall implantation tends towards an optimization of solar orientation and the distances between the volumes.

Given their independence and their interior distribution, then, the different volumetries seek to provide the finest quality possible to the general run of housing units, most of them facing south or southeast towards the good views: towers with balconied apartments and intermediary bar buildings with garden apartments and duplexes.

A conscientious dematerialization of the prismatic volumes is undertaken by way of setbacks, the handling of corners, bases, crowns and boundaries of all kinds.

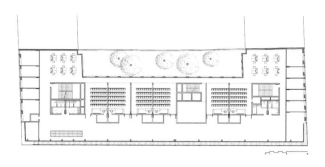

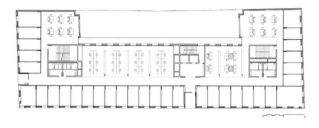

Typical floor plan

Lawyers Union Headquarters in Lyon

In the city of Lyon, Servient street has an urban potential that makes the plot of the former district archive building particularly interesting, located in the city center and close to the Palais de Justice and the Part Dieu station.

The first project decision was to enhance that urban multiplicity while responding to a highly mixed program with three uses: Law School, Bar Association and office spaces for rent.

The project chooses to avoid the opacity of some official buildings and aims instead to display the transparency of its activities. A private building, but with a public and institutional character, that shows its circulations and its programmatic horizontal division, and which becomes porous and accessible from the public space.

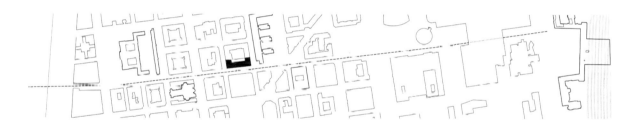

Architecture & Industry

Ceramic Materiality. Vila Real Public Library

The rectangular 40x17m plot oriented with its long side towards the northeast, consists of 4.685m2. It is situated between an important avenue of access to Vila-real and a school, and has a pre-existing, underground parking lot with exits and ventilation.

At the same time, the project is conceived in a way specifically and solely for the constraints of this productive urban context. The project values the urban integration of the piece, proposing a free public space that passes through the access ramps. The front plaza of the school is understood, after a first shaded area, as a void from which arise the plant embankments that situate and enhance the building. The checkerboard openings on both sides of the façade, and the possibility of cooling the south side of the building, allows the induction of adiabatic ventilation. The building features ventilation and natural lighting that minimize energy consumption while providing a luminous filter, recommended for reading, in response to the sustainability requirements.

The central atrium of the library is transformed into a more public space linking the avenue with the garden-square created in front of the school.

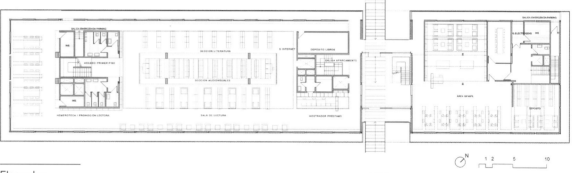

Floor plan

Working Spaces. Head Offices

Audiovisual Campus in 22@ District. Mediapro

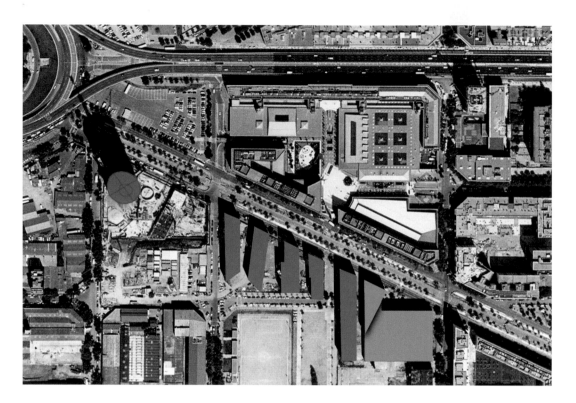

Carlos Ferrater

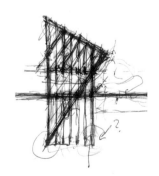

Building with steel

The evolution of architecture throughout time can be understood as a series of innovations in the way of building, and of new materials, which have enabled architects of different times to connect their ideological positions, intellectual challenges and technological advances with the search for new forms of expression.

Exposed steel skeletons became structural diagrams where it was possible to understand the relation of shear, bending, compression and traction, creating new aesthetics in which engineering and architecture turned cast iron and steel into a paradigm of modernity. Hidden skeletons, like that of Adler and Sullivan's Auditorium Building in Chicago, gave rise to standardised construction in order to create density in urban centres, defining a new city model and sacralising verticality as a new formal experience.

Mies van der Rohe rediscovered steel; he rigidified joints and gave rigour, order, proportion and meaning to the metal structural frame. His works in Chicago, New York and Berlin have a steel frame uniting and bringing timelessness to the classicism-modernity binomial, creating in the hidden part of the design process the conditions for the resulting materiality of his buildings.

Given its malleability, and versatility, its ability to support all sorts of shear and the ease with which it is used in construction, steel has also allowed a range of works to be erected masking absurd structures and arbitrary forms behind stone renderings and light metal and glass skins, to produce self-absorbed objects that do not respond to urban situations; they do not build a city; their functional programmes do not respond to proper social organisation and they exceed the limits of the shear-performance ratio, consuming excessive amounts of energy and adding expense to future maintenance requirements.

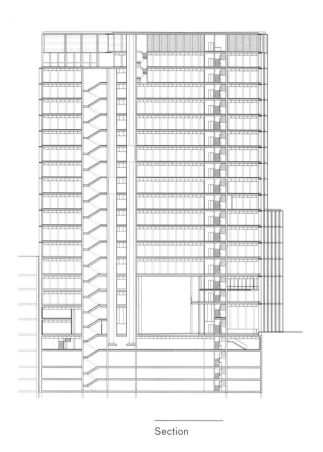

Section

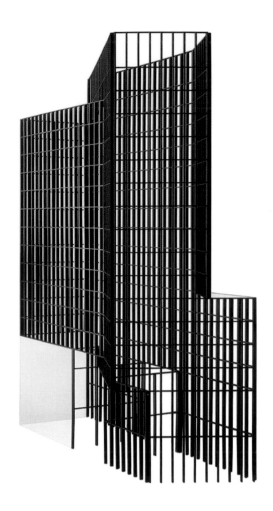

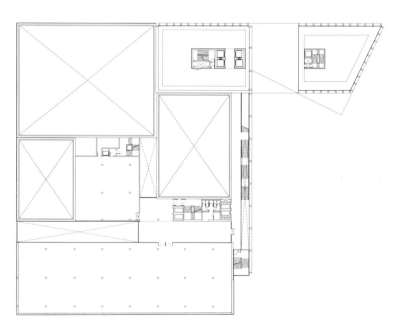

Ground floor plan

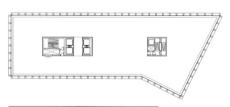

Typical plan of lower floor
with cantilevered overhang

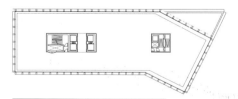

Typical plan of higher floor

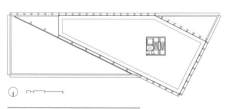

Presidential floor plan

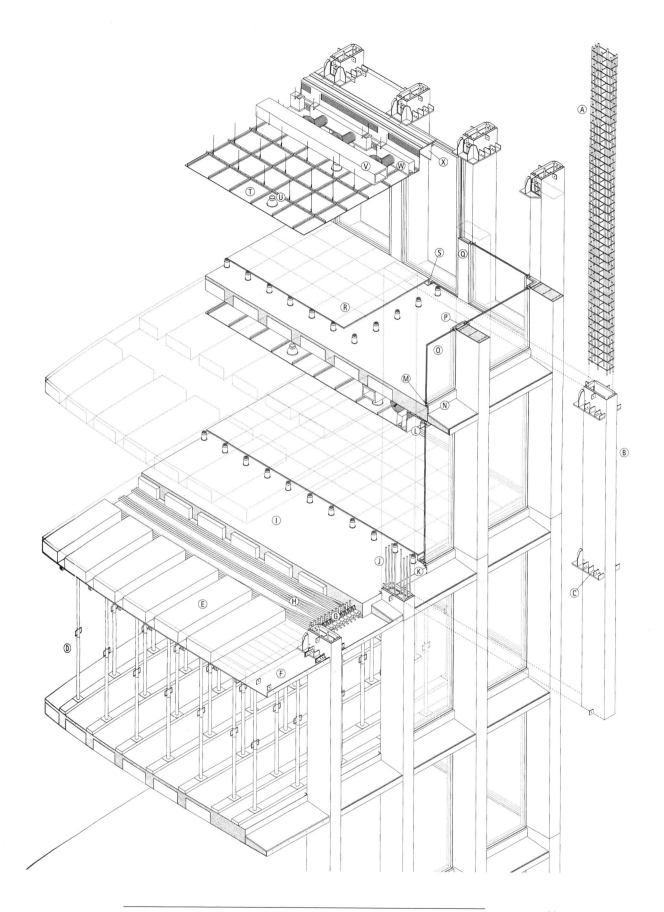

Structure and façade detail. Magazine extract *Tectónica* no.29. Steel (II)

Juan Calvo / Pondio Engineers

The stretch of Avinguda Diagonal that passes through 22@ District – the area of the city being reinvented hand in hand with new technologies – is marked by a sequence of buildings which, with the renowned Agbar tower as a backdrop, begins with the new headquarters of the Mediapro media group. Given its location, the design of the new building takes into special account the nature of its urban setting, and its volume has been modelled according to alignment and visual guidelines. Consequently, the main façade has been turned to face the avenue; the four first levels have been perforated to provide an opening for Carrer Bolivia and to direct interest to its perspective. On the lower level, the tower is diverted from the edge of the plot to create a new plane, allowing the adjacent building to be viewed.

These operations give a sculptural feel to the volume, intensified by the cantilevered tower and the resulting arris, and by the horizontal volume with a transparent façade that embraces the new triangular plaza.

The office tower's open plan design provides great flexibility of uses due to the absence of pillars and intermediate frames. The different floors have distinct layouts, allowing certain functional specialisation in their programmes that exceed the mere separation between the horizontal volume, which housed the audiovisual production and training centre, and the tower housing the company's administration.

The versatility of this interior layout is based on the use of a single and repeated window model, developed continuously on all of the façades. They offer good lighting conditions and views of the city from any point of the tower. The glass panes inside the grid stop glare and are protected from direct sun exposure, water and dirt.

The building's skeleton coincides with its final form owing to its perimeter frame. The grid of pillars on the façades and the slabs allow it to be considered a large Vierendeel truss, given that the fusion of membranes or structural diaphragms with the post-tensioned slabs make the large spans possible and provide the structure with rigidity. This system means that areas bearing less of the façade load collaborate to withstand the shear from the more tensioned parts of the grid in a kind of structural democracy. Finally, the greater height of the pillars on the lower levels and at the top – set aside for service installations – and the metallic bronze colour used in the structure and window frames give the building the solid and classic air of a great skyscraper.

The building already adopts sustainable forms from its urban setting alone, and the natural daylight received in all work areas is impeccable. The grid absorbs and spreads daylight uniformly. The structural design was made with strict environmental criteria. The large glazed expanses facing the public plaza are north-facing to avoid excessive exposure to the sun. The roof areas of the lower volume housing the film sets and production areas feature new generation solar panels.

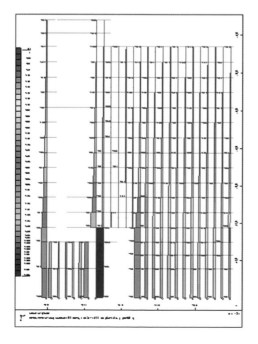

The façade contains 112 different pillar alignments. The perimeter of a standard floor has 74 pillars, separated by 1.90-2.05 m, according to the modular design of each façade.

They consist of an outer layer of thick steel plate filled with highly ductile concrete in order to increase their fire resistance time. They all have an external perimeter of 60x30 cm, with only the thickness of the steel wall varying depending on the load (some of them are of solid steel).

Each post-tensioned floor slab in the tower seems to be "sewn" with a series of 3 or 4-strand cables, each one made up of 3 or 4 Ø15-mm super-stabilised steel cables in a sheathe, designed to follow a course made up of straight lines and second-degree parabolas.

The tensioning process commences once the concrete has reached a typical resistance of 200Kp/cm^2, with a single tensioning stage of 20 Mp.

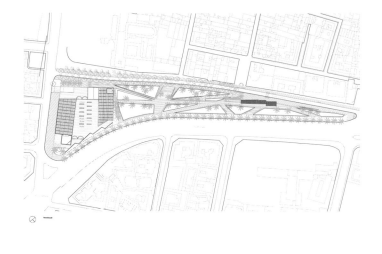

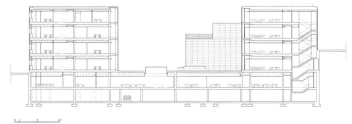

Corporate Headquarters for GISA & FGC

In one of the main entrances to Barcelona, integrated within the operation of covering over the FGC train tracks and the conversion of its former workshops, there appears a rectangular block resulting from the intersection of the urban weaves of the barrios of Sarriá and Tres Torres with Vía Augusta, thus generating a huge public space that will function as a hinge to resolve the height difference existing between the two barrios.

Emerging at the intersection of Vía Augusta with Calle Vergós and Calle Cardenal de Sentmenat is the group of buildings of the corporate headquarters of GISA and FGC, which notwithstanding the restrictiveness of the planning of the specific, pronounced volumetry stem from a work of urban integration, conferring on them a character typical of institutional buildings, a character at once emblematic, welcoming and functional.

The functional program of the two buildings is resolved by means of diaphanous floors giving onto the public space between them and of offices in the outer perimeters. The facade modulation is highly refined in order to give flexibility and versatility to the interior distribution.

A detailed plan with highly exacting constructional solutions resolves the exterior skin as a whole with a single module of extruded, anodized aluminum.

Hipodromo Tower

Office Building in Guadalajara. Mexico

The tower is located opposite Patria Avenue, near the crossing with Las Américas Avenue, on an irregular site at a different street level with respect to Hipódromo de Zapopán Street.

The project adapts the tower floor plan to the geometry of the plot, formally responding to the urban conditions of the site, like the nearby buildings and the front side facing the avenue, until it forms a slim volume, complex both in plan and in height, with a distinct top ending outlined against the sky.

The circulation and services core is centered, placed at the back of the site, articulating the two office areas on each floor.

The tower emerges from the ground over a concrete vase that adapts to the irregular geometry of the site while the parking levels are solved with sloping slabs that go down in a helicoidal path, and placing the parking spaces on the perimeter.

The building modular enclosure, formed by the structural concrete grid, is a double facade; the interior glazing, which enables the openings necessary for maintenance and ventilation, and the exterior one, composed of a thick square lattice built with glass-reinforced concrete that adapts to the structural grid openings.

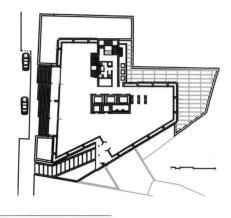

Ground floor plan

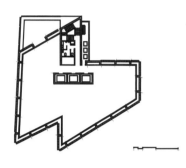

Typical floor plan

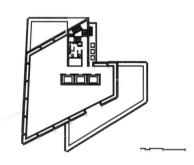

Top floor plan

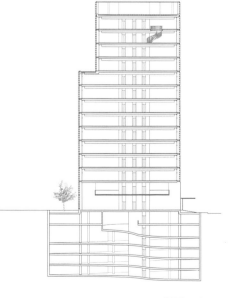

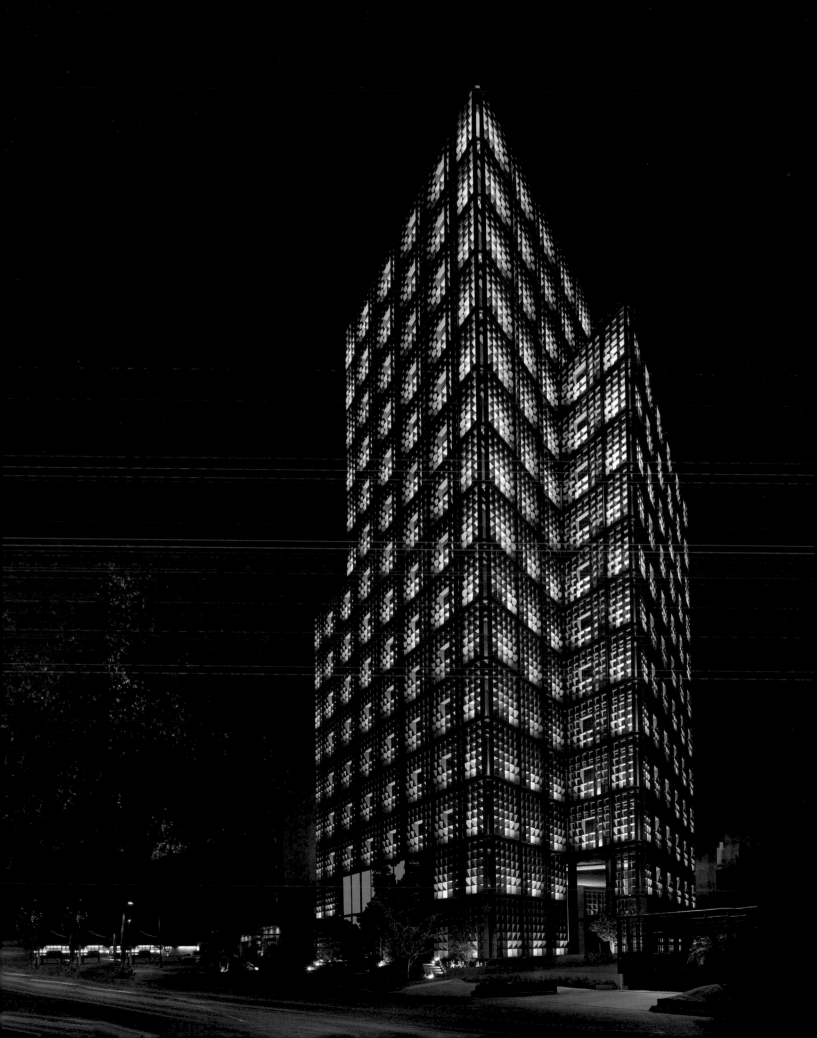

Interior Spaces with Identity

Borja Ferrater

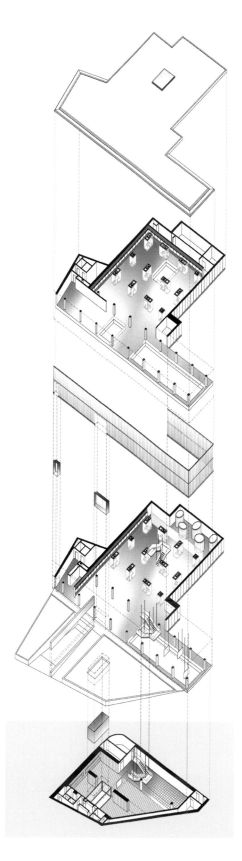

Finally, after considering different opportunities, a solution was reached for the façade based on the placement of a single material, a succession of multiple panes of glass placed perpendicularly to the axis of the façade. Tests and prototypes were used to confirm how to produce new effects such as diffraction, reflection and refraction of the light obtained as a result of the distortion, translation and overlaying of images through the façade.

Light, both daylight and artificial night illumination, became the predominant feature. We achieved a totally ambiguous façade that proved to be an element as solid in the day as it was liquid at night, as heavy as it was light, as rugged as it was smooth, and where it would be difficult at times to know if it was transparent, translucent or opaque. Consequently, when we look in from the outside, the façade offers us an ambiguous and distorted view of the building's interior, making it necessary to enter in order to discover what it is really like inside. Once inside, if we look out towards the city, we observe a series of visual effects, as if it were a game, where nothing is really where it should be. Some rays of light pass through in a straight line while others are reflected backwards, producing something similar to a superimposed image. At the same time, others are diffracted to show all the colours of the rainbow.

From the inside, we observe streets that were not there before; buildings are doubled, and we see pedestrians walking by and we think they are where we see them, while they are actually somewhere else. We fulfilled our aim of a façade that would offer different images of the same reality whenever one looked carefully through it. While designing a building projected towards the exterior, a unique world, space and atmosphere was sought for the interior.

On the inside, light, audiovisual installations, materials and exhibition elements were used to create an interior that was very distinct from a typical exhibition space, where the visitor could have an intense and unique experience with the building. Therefore, the interior space was designed as a personal and sensory experience where users or visitors could interact with the building by means of presence detectors, directional loudspeakers, light changes, projections, projected figures and plasma screens showing objects in movement. All of these elements appear to have been inserted, as if they were floating around an indivisible and continuous space. Slightly reflective and experimental ceramic flooring, a stainless steel suspended ceiling and expanded polystyrene foam tetrahedrons on the walls are the three predominant materials featured in the interior.

These are all continuous materials; in the form of three continuous planes they recreate a weightless space, emphasising horizontality and lacking in spatial or formal references. The physical space becomes a sort of virtual space. The idea of materiality dominates the building. All the materials used – laminated glass on the façade, stainless steel strips on the ceilings, foam rubber acoustic insulation pyramids and panels set over plywood strips on the walls and mosaic tiles on the floor – result in multiple joints that can be understood as continuous surfaces owing to the absence of perceivable joins. We could say that typical materials were used but transformed into new and singular ones. Technology applied to the building, the audiovisuals and the way of explaining the brand and its products is an essential part of conveying the company's commitment to the future. The Roca Barcelona Gallery project resonates with the most advanced lighting technology. For this ROCA and the architectural team at OAB (Borja, Lucía and Carlos Ferrater) worked together with a team of experts in such different fields as communications, lighting and audiovisuals, and many other specialists who have made it possible to create an original buidling and an emblem for the brand.

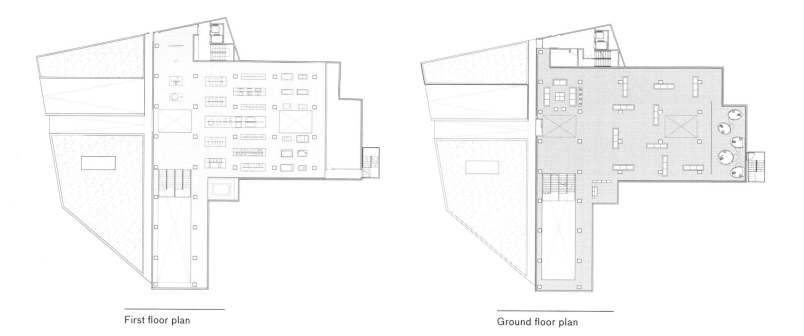

First floor plan

Ground floor plan

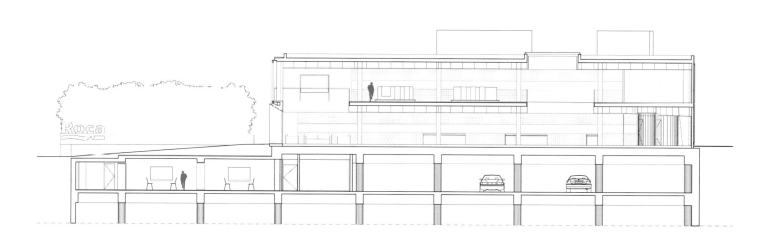

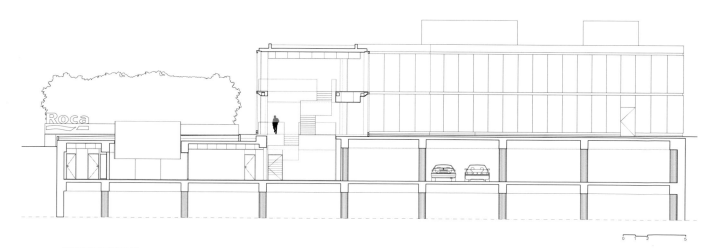

Sections

Cocina Hermanos Torres Restaurant

The Cocina Hermanos Torres is a project born from the desire to create a new experience with regard to the culinary and restaurant world. An innovative space that serves to embody an original dining adventure. The building and its interior design unite in pursuit of a unique encounter.

"More than a restaurant with a kitchen, we would like to create a kitchen with a restaurant" is the premise of the Torres brothers when beginning the transformation of a former 800 m2 industrial warehouse, which had to be totally remodeled, to become "the ship of dreams." The project, carried out by the OAB studio of Carlos and Borja Ferrater, was therefore born with the desire to remove or reduce some dividing lines between the different spaces that make up a traditional restaurant, placing the kitchen not only as the central operational element, but also as an enveloping one. The restaurant is the kitchen as well as the performance stage where the diner is the audience as well as the lead actor.

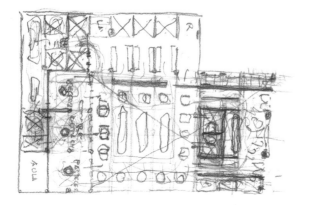

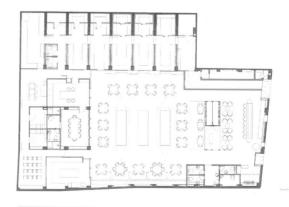

Floor plan

Waterfronts

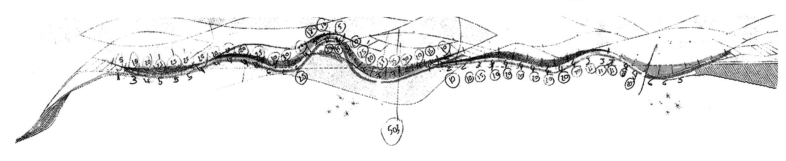

Benidorm West Beach Promenade

The promenade in Benidorm, a new transitional location between built city and the natural space of sea and beach.

The promenade is not understood as a frontier/borderline but as an intermediary space rendering this transition permeable.

It is structured as a place with a rich topography, as a dynamic space that accommodates the act of strolling and watching the sea, but also organises different areas for stopping and relaxing in.

The promenade subsumes the longitudinal and transverse flows of the different circulations and channels these, allowing easy access to the beach. It eliminates architectural barriers, permitting direct access from parking places.

The promenade thus becomes an architectonic location that molds a new topography and plays with light and shade.

A nexus of sinuous interwoven lines which sets up the different spaces and adopts various natural and organic shapes evocative of the fractal structure of a cliff, as well as the motion of waves and tides.

The promenade is structured in different layers: a first structural layer creates the perimeter line in white concrete; another textured layer with paving in different colors; and a last layer of street furniture and natural features like water and vegetation. All these contribute to a homogeneous location with its own personality; as well as being a predecessor to the new architecture of the
21st century by combining building technology and nature in one ensemble.

The new Benidorm promenade is put forward, then, as a new form, one integrating the artificial (or built) and the natural.

The project subsumes three different essences within the organic forms of modernism: the forms of fractal geometry in nature; the latest building technologies; and avant-garde landscape design.

The new promenade leaves nothing to chance but grows out of setting up a number of specific laws, a geometrical ground plan and modulation. A constructional logic is thus established, facilitating its modulation in sections.

The beach partly invades zones previously occupied by the former esplanade, increasing the surface area of sand and reducing that of asphalt.

All the functional aspects are brought together: the promenade, rest and relaxation area, vantage point, transition to the beach, architectural barriers, direct access to parking, rainwater collectors, beach lighting, road communication, integration of street furniture, services infrastructure, and so on.

A new landside frontage is constructed, providing views of the sea and the beach from the upper level of the promenade, and a new borderline established, integrating the different circulations in its undulations and platforms, eliminating a barrier and constructing a place for people to be in.

Section

Final elevation

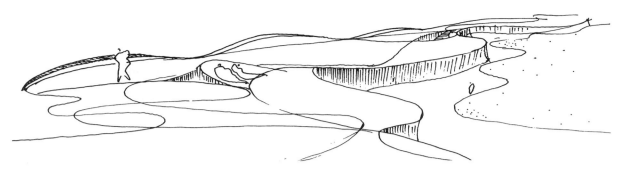

Xavier Martí i Galí

The Benidorm urban development model has been criticised for years for its appearance, owing to it being out of keeping; for its choice of encouraging high-rise buildings; for overcrowding and land speculation; for its excessive density; and for its lack of public and community spaces other than its splendid beach.

50 years have passed since that decision taken by the council, and seen now in comparison with the different tourist resorts on the Spanish coast faced with the systematic destruction of the coastline with invasive residential complexes, poor waterfront areas, immense ghost towns that are empty most of the year and which require a consequent effort to maintain infrastructure, roads, services and security, etc. one must wonder whether the Benidorm model in fact turned out to be the most "sustainable" one on the Spanish coast. It occupies very little land, no more than a few hectares, and there is very little use of private transport as everywhere in the town is only a 10-minute walk away from the beach. Most inhabitants have a sea view from their towers. A special feature of the construction involved not sealing the land under asphalt, owing to the respect for the original sloping topography which keeps the natural rainwater channels among the gardens surrounding the apartment tower blocks. There are more than 500,000 people accommodated here during seasonal peaks and the tourist season is year round.

This was the perspective we had with Carlos Ferrater for our participation in the invitation-only design competition for the West Beach promenade, where we considered the possibility of radically restricting vehicular traffic along the waterfront and designing 1.5 km of promenade with a maximum width of 30 m, with a series of overhangs that would not reduce the surface area of the sand and which would be possible because of the 3-4-metre slope between the town and the beach. This would give rise to a large public leisure space that would bring the town into contact with the sea and provide a new seaside promenade for the use of residents and tourists. This new place with such a privileged position between the town and the beach would become a transition space, the border between two worlds.

Benidorm now has a natural space built using a sustainable project fused with technology, craftwork using local materials in the Mediterranean sun.

It would be a place for imagination evoking other projects such as that by Clorindo Testa in Mar del Plata and that by Roberto Burle Marx in Rio de Janeiro.

The technical and architectural considerations leading to the Benidorm West Beach Promenade responded to a model tying together the cultural characteristics of the place with the intellectual concepts that have been developed inside our practice in recent years. Therefore, the sustainability of the project could be understood as going beyond the application of technological devices to the project. On the contrary, it would arise from the actual qualities of the location (hedonism, leisure, popular traditions, the imprint left by the waves), assimilated by means of a theoretical design that is upheld with the application of geometry to the landscape. This contributed to the first, and perhaps the most important, environmental condition of a project, that of being designed and built using culturally-sustainable criteria.

The technical and architectural considerations leading to the Benidorm West Beach Promenade responded to a model tying together the cultural characteristics of the place with the intellectual concepts that have been developed inside our practice in recent years. Therefore, the sustainability of the project could be understood as going beyond the application of technological devices to the project. On the contrary, it would arise from the actual qualities of the location (hedonism, leisure, popular traditions, the imprint left by the waves), assimilated by means of a theoretical design that is upheld with the application of geometry to the landscape. This contributed to the first, and perhaps the most important, environmental condition of a project, that of being designed and built using culturally-sustainable criteria.

Geometry and sustainable construction: the concrete membrane

Experimentation with form led to a series of building processes in this project that specifically responded to its qualities, but which also responded to the general laws governing the relation between form and function: The alveolar geometry of the concrete membrane gave the form rigidity, allowing us to reduce the thickness of the concrete layer to only 10 centimetres, which not only significantly reduced the amount of material used, but also made it easy to use, shortening building times. Likewise, the geometric configuration of the slab dissipates the energy of the wind and sea as it does not behave with the rigidity of a continuous wall, which would act as a barrier.

The overhangs resulting from the geometry enabled the surface area of the promenade to be increased by 4,000m² without impacting on the surface of the beach, turning the areas protected by them into shady spaces that have been greatly appreciated by beachgoers.

Together with the white concrete, the membrane geometry enhances light, reducing the intensity of lighting required from street lamps, resulting in lower energy costs and demand. Therefore, the need for minimal lighting to provide good illumination not only contributes to lower energy use but light pollution over the beach is also reduced owing to the effects of light on the wall. Consequently, efficient lighting contributed to the environmental sustainability of the project.

The minimalist design of luminaires, railings and benches, which also permit chairs to be incorporated, helped to minimise the use of materials, costs, construction, assembly and maintenance. Plant cover was also improved through the use of native plants and by recycling the pre-existing palm trees, as they are suited to the climate found here.

It is worth mentioning that the variety of forms presented in the project along the length of its 1,500 metres was achieved using differential standardisation. The resulting form was obtained using 55 moulds each with a 5.15-metre lineal length. Owing to alterations in the layout of the moulds, a differential configuration was achieved that produced the different geometries that can be appreciated along the length of the project.

This type of flexibility can also be appreciated in the paving tiles designed for the promenade. The glazed coloured stoneware tiles, developed in collaboration with the ALICER Ceramic Technology Institute and produced by Keramia, adapts to the formal and topographical needs of the project. From a formal perspective, being circular, the tile geometry does not emphasise any particular directionality, facilitating its placement and allowing interchanged use of coloured tiles throughout the interwoven design on the pavement. From at topographic perspective, the tiles adapt to the different changes in level, removing the need for complementary tiles.

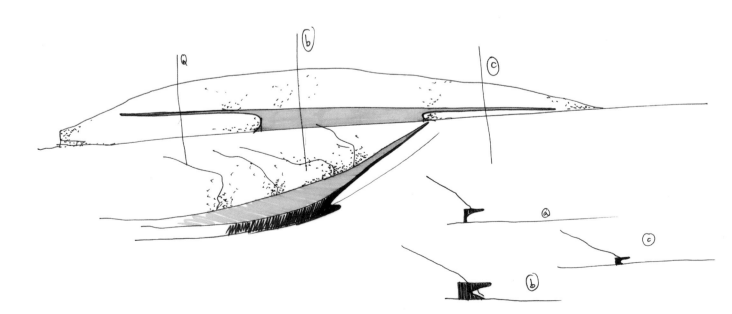

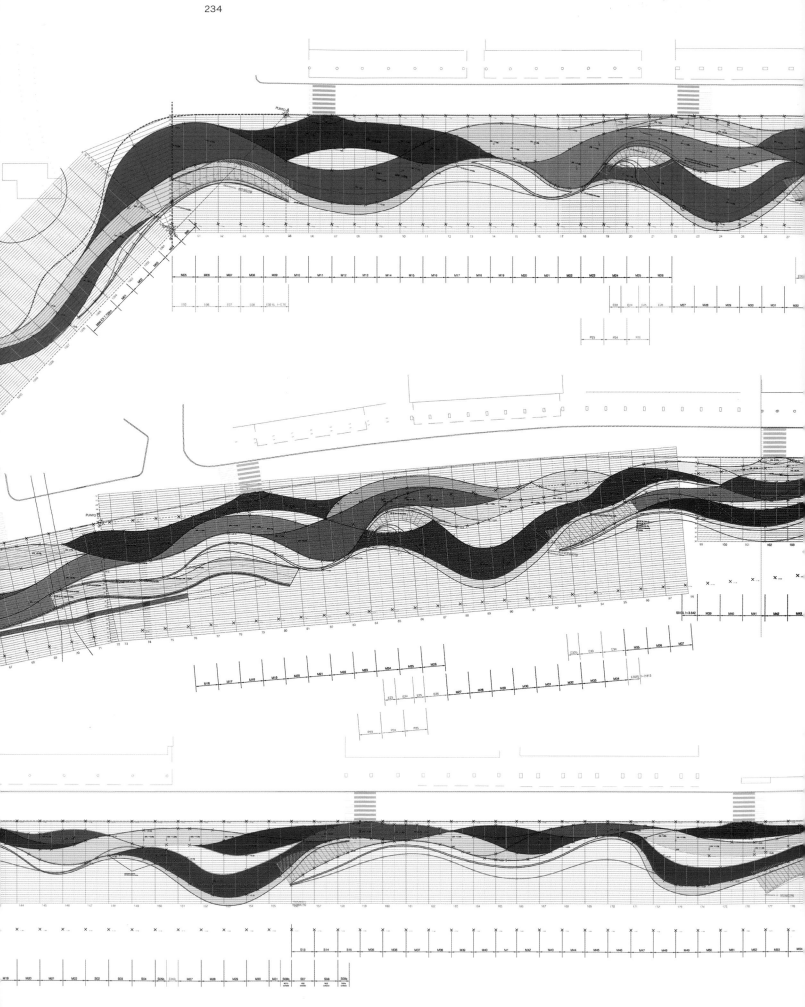

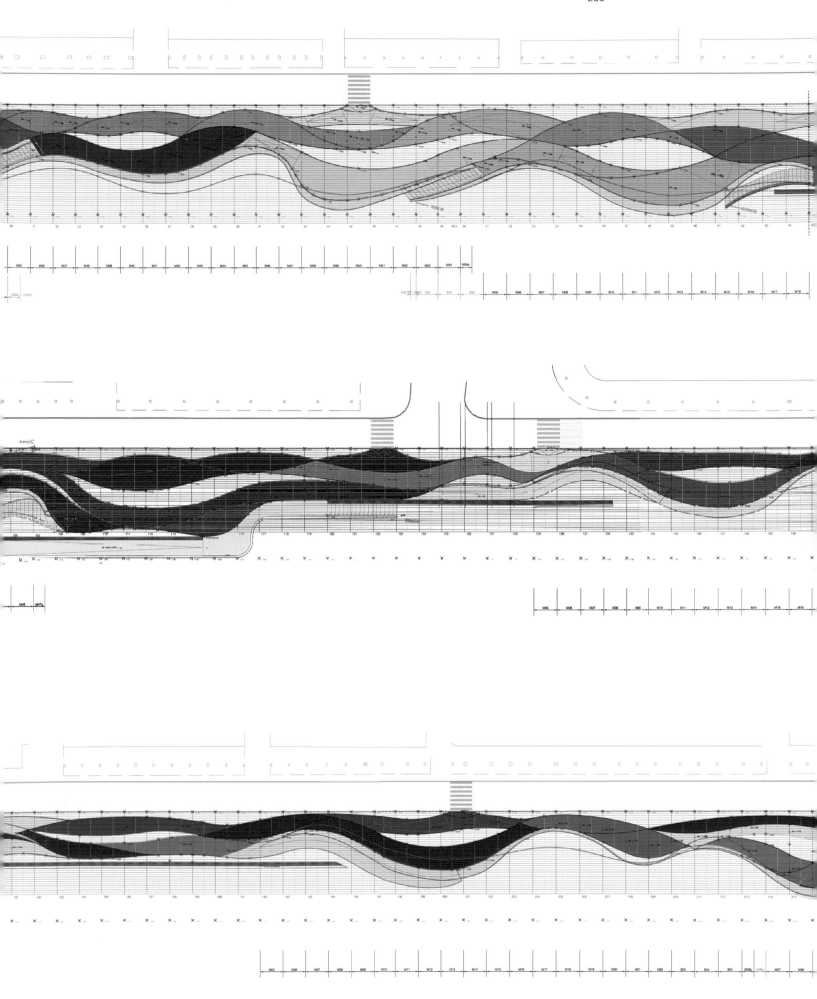

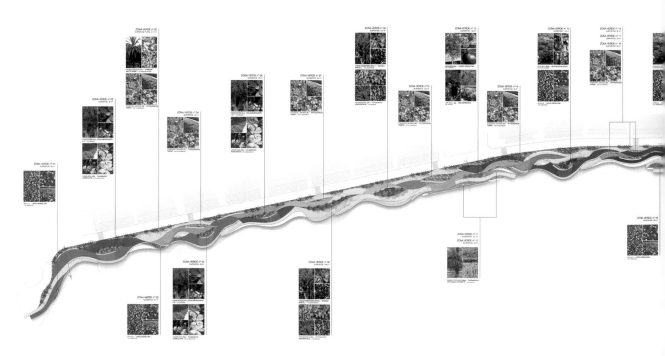

Vegetation plan

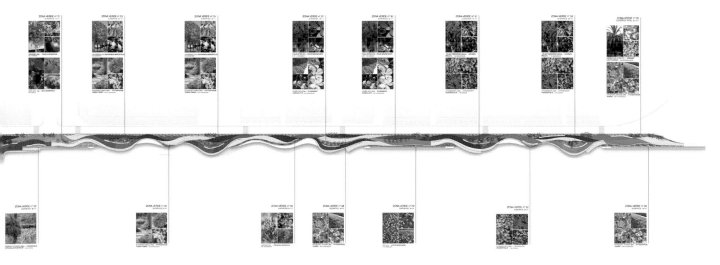

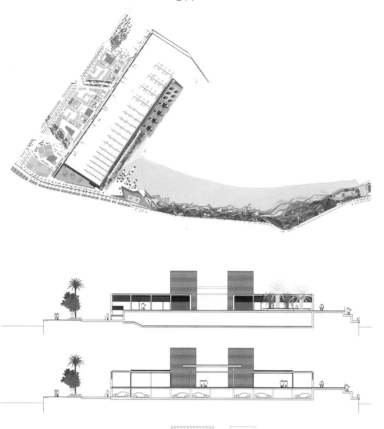

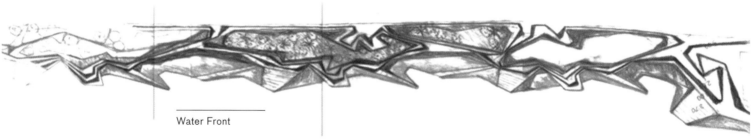

Pleisance Dock Sections

Water Front

Tanger Waterfront

The project for the Corniche de Tanger brings together certain concepts researched and experimented by OAB in two previous projects, the Barcelona Botanical Garden with its grid of pathways, reinforced earth walls, and vegetation communities in a maritime climate, and the cantilevers in the Benidorm seafront promenade, a topography which unfolds between the city and the sea with ceramic pavements and colors typical of the place, and furniture elements and native vegetation that complete the intervention.

The new "corniche" promenade in Tangier provides a backbone for the seaside districts, residential areas and popular sport facilities, preserving the natural conditions of the maritime geography.

The solution for the new marina and leisure port is completed with the plaissance buildings; bars, restaurants, sailing clubs and leisure zones. The berth borders are detached and floating in order to preserve the public use of the water while at the same time addressing the tide issue.

The buildings on the marina dock are built with lightweight concrete structures and lattices.

Control tower in Tanger waterfront

Water Front Barcelona

The Fish Market in Barcelona's Port

The building for the new Fish Market of Barcelona attempts to reorganize the current Barcelona dock and the Balear dock between the fishing net warehouse and the Clock Tower, formerly the lighthouse at the old port entrance.

A ramp and a footbridge at a height of 4,5 m solve the visitor access at a raised level, from where they can watch the movements of both the white fish and blue fish fleets, follow the auctions and enjoy the bars and restaurants without disturbing the work of the fishermen and the auction bidders.

The building consists of three volumes that house different uses, offices and auction halls, blue fish handling naves and ice factory and canteen.

The black concrete column and beam structure and the ribbed aluminum sheet panels in the exterior envelope, will enable an appropriate maintenance and guarantee long-term durability.

View of the Old Fish Market
from the New's one under construction

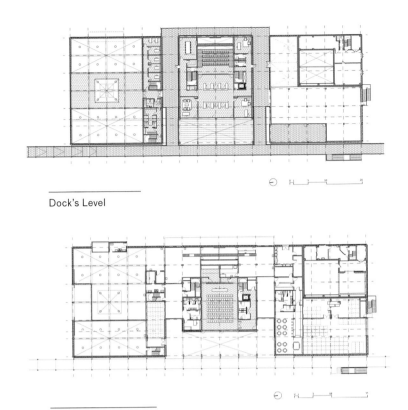

Dock's Level

First floor Level

Horizonscrapers

Carlos Ferrater

The eastern side of Montjuïc facing the Ronda del Litoral and the port has a steep cliff and a profile degraded by erosion. It passes between the beautiful cemetery and the themed gardens of Costa i Llobera. You could say that it is the contrasting section or the extrados of the Botanical Garden's transept.

The actual geology of the stone of Montjuïc, its almost vertical section and coastal horizon, encouraged me to apply for the international with competition in which Barcelona City Council requested a solution to "els cims de muntanya de Montjuïc" to literally attach a group of buildings to the mountainside at different heights using cantilever construction in which different activities had to be located: from a centre of worship next to the cemetery, programmes for city and port facilities, to horizontal structures to support the gardens as an extension of those existing in the Eastern sector.

The term "rascahorizontes" (horizonscrapers) known more commonly as "rasca-suelos" (landscrapers) challenges the term skyscrapers, although from a structural point of view they have a similar root. Both are two cantilevered corbels subjected mainly to the lateral force of the wind as the weight of a skyscraper creates a smaller force compared to buckling due to slenderness or horizontal forces.

We had to make the most of the stone support of the mountain as had to be done in Manhattan with the granitic subsoil to find structural mechanisms that made it possible for bracket structures to perform efficiently. With the help of Juan Calvo, our regular co-worker, we devised a system that would strain the upper part of the large central support beam making it work in tension and tighten deep anchorages while the lower section was compressed against the rock mass distributed over a large surface. A ring system distributed throughout the large central bracket helps to distribute the force while the outer shell that forms the living areas of the building is reinforced. All the installation networks and services are located longitudinally inside this large central beam while an exterior linear corridor is embedded and suspended in the lower section of the "horizonscraper" resolving the escape route that continues along the emergency staircases which are also suspended. A large column contains the lifts that ascend from the base of the mountain acting as a strut that secures the cantilever.

Montjuïc lift. Barcelona's gateway from the sea

The construction of a lift is proposed, passing under the viaduct of Barcelona's coastal ring road, that would pick up visitors from cruise ships and the Port as well as bus and coach passengers from the ring road itself. A stop would also be provided on the sharp bend in the road that goes up to Miramar. All of them would access the gates of the castle via a final walkway, from where they could visit the different facilities, parks and gardens on the hill at Montjuïc.

It would also be possible to create an intermediate stop that would lead to Barcelona's old lighthouse which has already been renovated.

Two large 100-person elevators, surrounded by three staircases, would allow easy access to the upper level and a safe evacuation route.

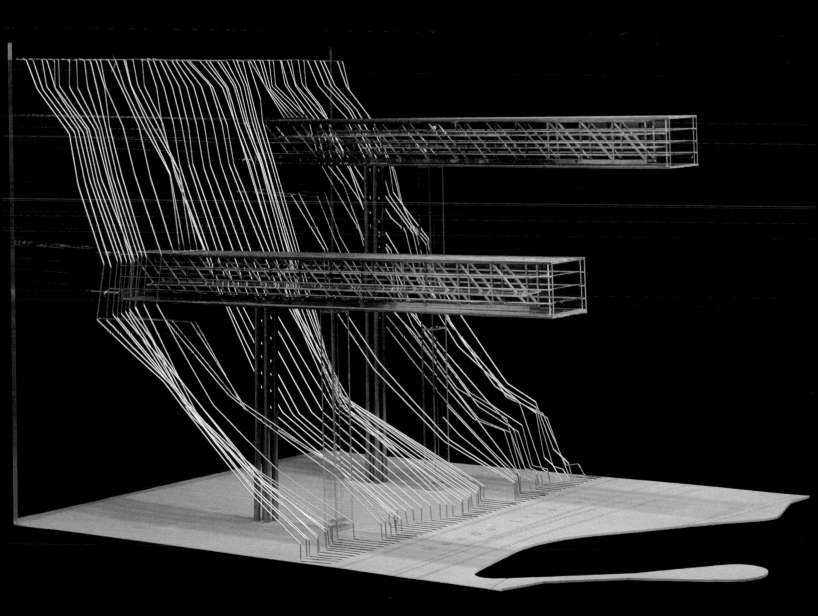

Horizonscrapers

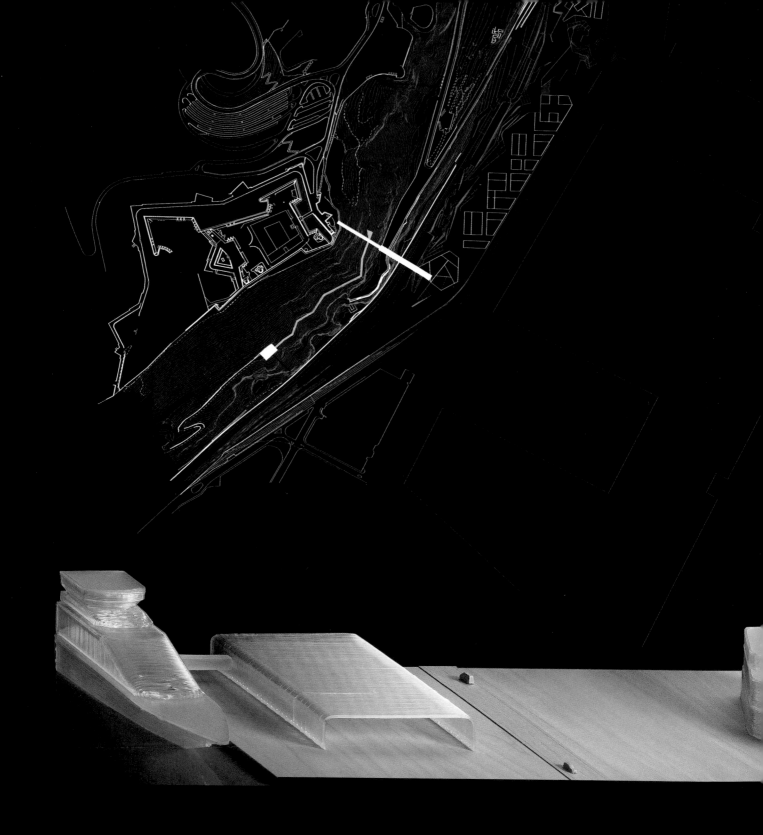

Climbing from the port to the Montjuic Castle

Social Housing

In a enclave close to the city of Barcelona we develop a building with 108 public housing apartments. On the ground floor, an autonomous commercial space and the pedestrian access is via two central communication cores. These cores link the city level with the upper platform level, thanks to an interior pedestrian street which leads to the communal area at the back via patios and landscaped pathways. The volumetric scheme is resolved by means of 3 seemingly freestanding towers, which go to form the main frontage on avenue. Theses are bonded to a slightly lower linear block that acts as a backdrop to the building complex. The volumes are united in the central empty space by the communication cores. This layout permits all the apartments to be oriented towards the south and with views of the city, and to profit from such eco-efficient passive measures as natural light and cross-ventilation. The 3 towers emphasize their verticality thanks to their composition. By dematerializing the corners and creating transparency in the foreshortened view, the poetic image of the Miesian skyscraper is evoked.

From the point of view of materiality and given the limited budget, a studied modulation and a combination of continuous single-layer white facings with the presence of a noble material like aluminum

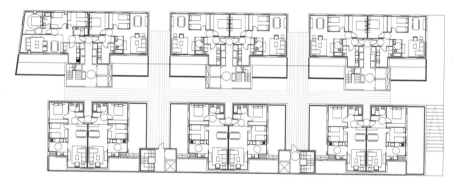

Platform Level

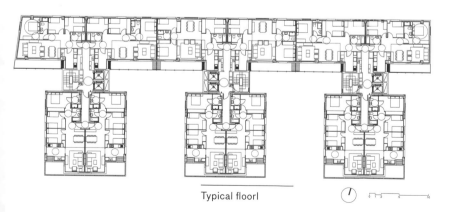

Typical floorl

Social housing in Villaverde, Madrid sur

The project proposes the construction of a building which respects the particular conditions of an irregularly shaped plot, a program of apartments with different surface areas, a complicated set of planning regulations, and a complex urban implantation.

The building is divided into two bodies:
The first body, in which the vertical communications core is found, is a (GF + 8) tower, trapezoidal in shape, which adapts to the alignments of the road system by being set back on the two upper floors. Located within it are the apartments of 70 m² (three bedrooms) and of 60 m² (two bedrooms).

The second body or block building is separated from the first by an atrium patio which spans the plot longitudinally; in this way the exterior stairway of the tower building articulates the two volumes by spanning the patio with a bridge on the third floor. Three stories high, this second body contains the 90-m² apartments: four duplexes with private gardens on the ground level, with access from the patio, and two apartments on the third floor.

With this volumetric distribution we arrive at maximum usability of the plot in terms of the number of apartments and of their quality, while respecting the planning regulations currently in force.

The final volumetry helps structure the entrances from the street, the vehicles' access ramp to the parking lot and the private garden area.

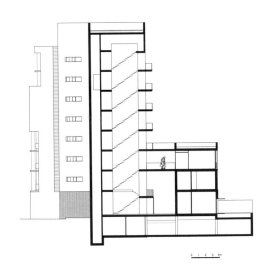

Housing and inhabitants

Carlos Ferrater

House for Photographer 2

A plot perpendicular to the sea measuring 250 m in length by 18 m in width.
The piece of land lies in an agricultural area that runs back from the beach to a place that forms a backdrop of old ruins, reeds and lemon trees.

The Home for Photographer 2 stands at the back of the site. Built on a platform raised 50 cm over the floodable natural terrain, three small volumes with irregular layouts and elevations create a dialogue through a void with visual distractions.

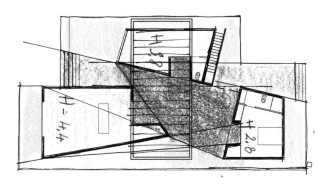  

La fàbrica d'Horta
(Factory in Horta), 1909
Pablo Picasso

A grove of 51 Washingtonia palms leads from the beach to the house.
The deconstructed volumes adapt to the conditions of the landscape, of buildings and light that suggest a painting by Picasso that was painted in the area and now hangs in the Picasso Museum in Paris.

The central void becomes the main space of the home, a tense space geometrically composed in its upper part through the tall, opaque structures of the different pavilions and from the ground up to a height of 2.10 m on a continuous site where the different shaded interior spaces are connected with views of the sea, the lush backdrop and the living areas on the platform.

The set of deconstructed volumes reminds us of Picasso's cubist work. The chiaroscuro and the intense light of this area of the Mediterranean balance the flat landscape of this area of the Ebro Delta.

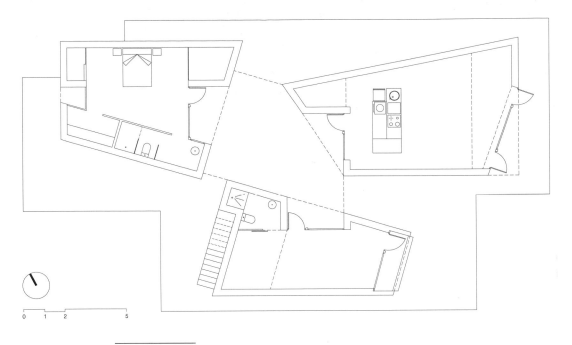

Floor plan

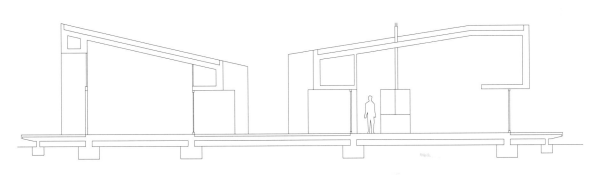

Section

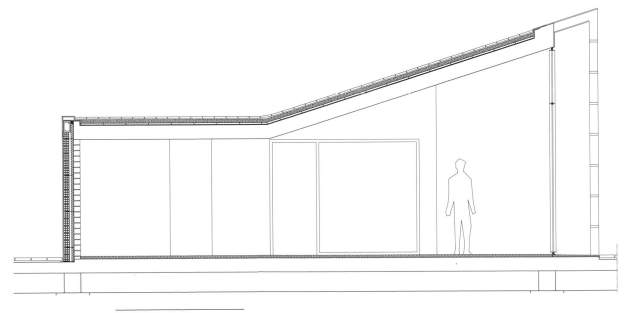

Construction section

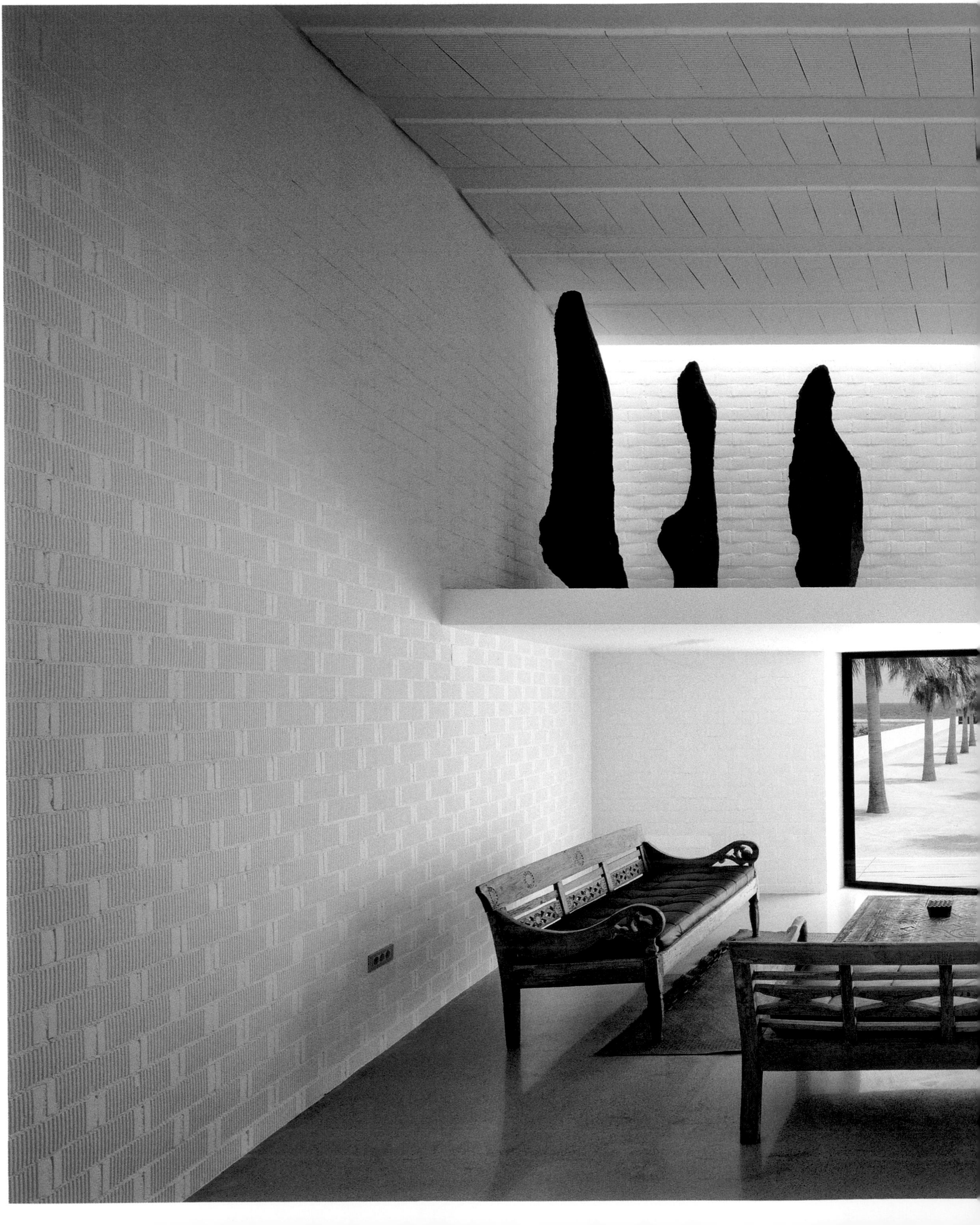

Photo by José Manuel Ferrater

Lucía Ferrater   Xavier Martí Galí

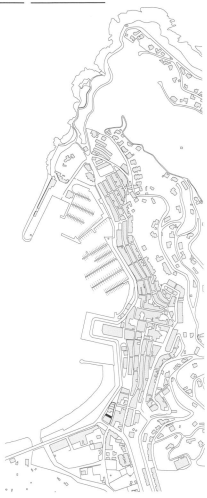

Seafront house in Port de la Selva

The house is situated on Port de la Selva Bay, on the northern coast of Cap de Creus Natural Park, with its face to the sea and the Tramuntana wind.

A building between party walls, the house takes account of the cultural legacy of the location and draws its inspiration from the F. Correa and A. Milá's Villavecchia House and J.A. Coderch's Senillosa House, both of them in the neighboring village of Cadaqués, these being examples of a respect for the traditional while incorporating conveniences and features of the modern.

The house is constructed on a deep, narrow plot of land between two streets, Passeig de la Plaja and Calle Selva de Mar, with taller buildings extremely close by.

The section resolves the conditions imposed by the regulations to do with the historic center by being stepped as it nears the street to the back, thereby improving conditions of insolation and ventilation and tailoring the upper reaches as traditional façades of the protected patios.

In constructional terms, the house is resolved by economizing on its means and by recognizing the internal structural logic of its materials, which thanks to the angle of entry of the light point up the more sensitive aspects of its interior.

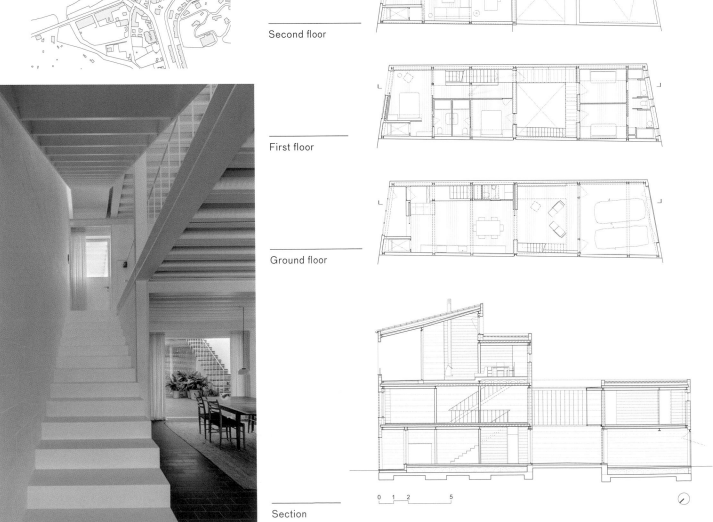

Second floor

First floor

Ground floor

Section

0 1 2   5

Pineda House

Faced with the challenge of building a single-family house on a long, narrow piece of land with a height difference of more than 22 meters, we began the design process by trying to understand the needs of its residents.

The house is meant for a family from abroad; he, a Norwegian screenwriter, and she, a Mexican anthropologist specializing in primates. From the start both of them emphasized the year-long need to receive family and friends from all over the world. The twin objective of not overdensifying the volume as a whole and of laying it out in two parts along the land lot permitted us to fragment the volume and also to grant privacy and autonomy to the guest pavilion.

The house is built of bare concrete with an application of white toner. Inside, austere finishes are proposed, with Catalan ceramic units used for the flooring.

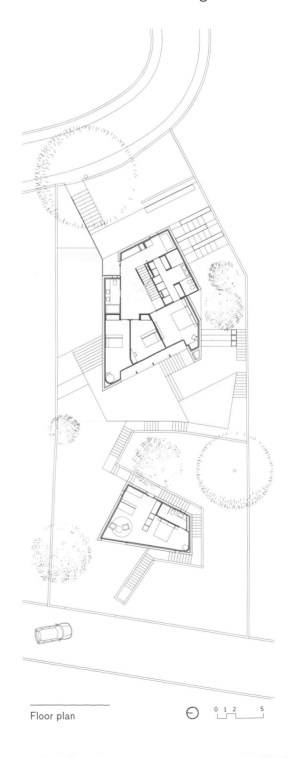

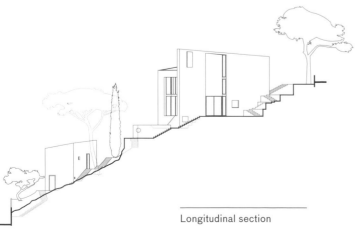

Longitudinal section

Floor plan

0 1 2 5

L'Escala

"From Mar d'en Manassa to Port d'en Perris"

Note from the mayor of L'Escala:
"Ferrater has suggested an idea for the seafront at L'Escala, from Mar d'en Manassa
to Port d'en Perris, giving it back its old original essence."

Pacification of the L'Escala seafront

On to the small party-wall house built by my parents in the 1960s, I projected a space that takes advantage of the height allowed by the slope of the roof.

The real window consists of a large sheet of glass set back towards the interior. This constructs an intermediate space, allowing a perforation of the facade wall to frame the view towards the Gulf of Roses.

The seafront reformation comes from the idea of enhancing the natural attributes of the town of L'Escala: its unique geography, the Norfeu cape, Roses bay, the mountains in the background, amidst which the emblematic Canigó, the village of Sant Martí d'Empúries, the beaches, the ruins of the ancient city of Emporium and the view of the seafront itself, the beach with Cargol rock, Port d'En Perris and the promenade.

All this makes one of the most beautiful natural amphitheatres in the world. The project seeks to restore the tradition and ancient culture of a maritime location of great personality and character.

The project covers, enhances and highlights all these geographical, natural and historical attributes through absence, by eliminating all those elements that distort the site's quality.

The new Seafront from Mar d'en Manassa to Port d'en Perris

Urban Hotels
Barcelona and Ibiza

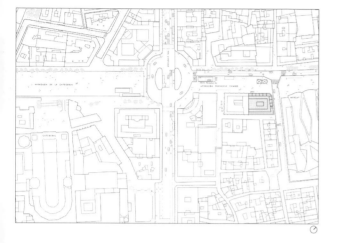

Situation

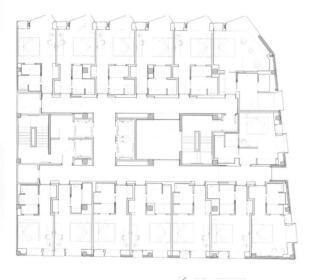

Typical floor plan

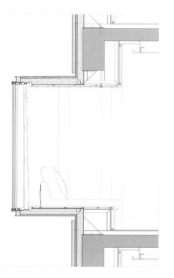

Facade detail

The Barcelona Edition Hotel

Situated opposite the old medieval market squarein the Santa Caterina neighborhood, the project consolidates the urban transformation of Ciutat Vella, which has led to the modernization of the historic center of Barcelona begun in the 1980s, while meeting the requirements of the operator of the new Barcelona Edition hotel, Ian Schrager, creator in the 1970s of New York's iconic Studio 54.

The new project posits a change of use for the existing office building, along with complete rehabilitation of the spaces within, by building a new skin that results from the tension between the new typology and the urban spaces surrounding the building.

The design for the hotel responds to this dual nature. On the one hand the ground floor with its double-height openings provides continuity with, and complements, the commercial activity of the market. On the other, the volumetry and the outer skin are modulated in a different way, as per the singularities of the urban fabric and their immediate public space.

The black ceramic skin with large-format panels constructs the vented, sustainable (Leed Gold) façade with open joints that accentuate a segmentation which calibrates the different apertures on each façade.

A huge oculus in the suites of floor 8 and 9 looks out over the roofing of the market, in a search, once again, for an interrelationship with the neighboring public space.

Interior Design: Rosa-Violán

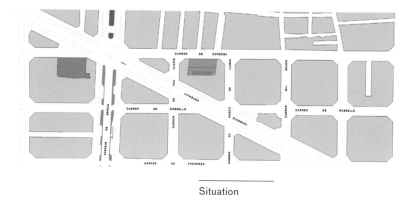

Situation

Typical floor plan

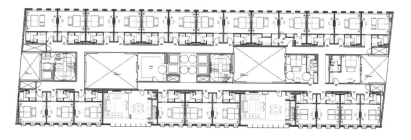

Elevation Carrer Còrsega

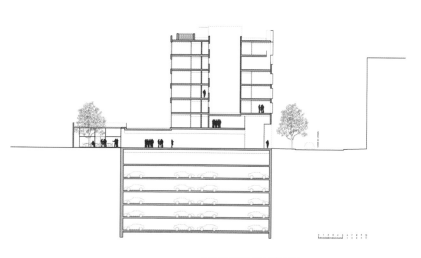

Cross section

Hotel Seventy in Barcelona

It is a large building on a site between dividing walls, with its main facade in Carrer Còrsega, within the urban fabric of the Eixample.

To achieve it, we came up with three different types of facade corresponding to different conditioning factors in their closest surroundings: the Carrer Còrsega facade, the facade looking inside the block, and the hotel courtyard facades.

The facade breaks down into two planes, one in glass and the other ceramic.

On the main facade, the openings project outwards from the plane in the form of brass boxes, creating an interplay of light and shade which reduces the screen effect of the building, achieving better proportion with the scale of the city.

Along the same lines, the two large galleries recall the skyline of the old Bayer factory.

At night, these boxes light up, looking as if they are floating on a black canvas. These mechanisms help to break down the longitudinal view of the facade, which occupies almost the whole block.

On the ground floor, the structure of the double-height metal doorways helps to construct a base that seeks a view of the internal garden and provides the building with presence.

The facade here is planned in the opposite way, this time with set-back glass, achieving up to 1 m depth from the base to the crown.

The facade recognises its visuals in perspective and emerges from this with the greatest possible advantage, with thickness and shadows which simplify the complexity to integrate it into its surroundings.

The rear facade, with carpentry also in the internal plane, generates an interplay of spaces, and groups the first two floors in a single void to obtain greater verticality.

The internal courtyards of the hotel take on particular importance, not only offering ventilation to some of the simpler rooms but also opening up to the internal distribution corridors.

To resolve the possibility of interference of visuals between corridors and rooms, a skin of vertical metal tubes has been constructed in the shape of a diamond, solving the problem in the form of large curtains.

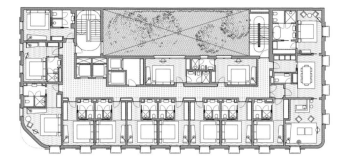

Typical floor plan

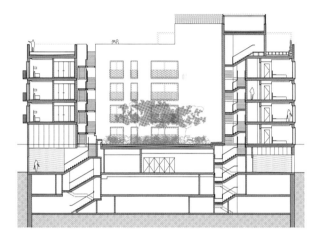

Cross section

The Standard Ibiza Hotel

The new boutique hotel belonging to the Standard chain stands in an urban area in Paseo Vara del Rey, opposite Dalt Vila, and shares a block with the iconic and historic Montesol Hotel. It completes the central section of the city of Ibiza, an area strictly protected as a World Heritage Site.

A white wall facade is proposed, curving at the intersections of Paseo Vara del Rey with Calle Ramón y Cajal and Ramón y Cajal with Calle Bartomeu Vicente Ramón. A single opening in the facade measuring 1.20 m wide by 2.30 m high extends into an open balcony with a 0.80 m overhang. Sliding shutters made of wooden slats cross the railings. Detached from the wall, they create a play of shadows on its white surface while preventing dirt and deterioration on the facade. All this interplay evokes the vernacular architecture of Ibiza: the white wall, the traditional openings, and the combination of the three materials that have always defined a traditional balcony – metal railings, glazed openings and wooden shutters.

Interior Design: Rosa-Violán

Ignacio Paricio is the author of the book Landscape Geometry, in which he shows the search for an internal structure in the geometries of the work of Carlos Ferrater and the OAB. His research analyses its role in creating and elaborating projects.

The results of his analysis show a common syntax, as well as the capacity of geometry to evolve towards new forms of architectural expression.

In his classification, Paricio establishes a synthesis of the various geometries, from the simplest to the most complex. He concludes by saying that most of the latter groups arise from the Botanical Garden project, the seed of the latest innovations in form.

"Geometric Taxonomy" in the work of Carlos Ferrater and OAB. Published by ACTAR in 2021.

— Simple shapes: manipulation of simple bodies. The combinations of these simple shapes are subdivided into two sections, juxtapositions and twins.

— Secondly, he discovers the geometrical voids in simple shapes. These, in turn, are subdivided into central and peripheral voids.

— Thirdly, he classifies the more complex geometries into two types: irregular and geometric.

— Finally, he constructs a new group based on the displacement of lines on a generatrix.

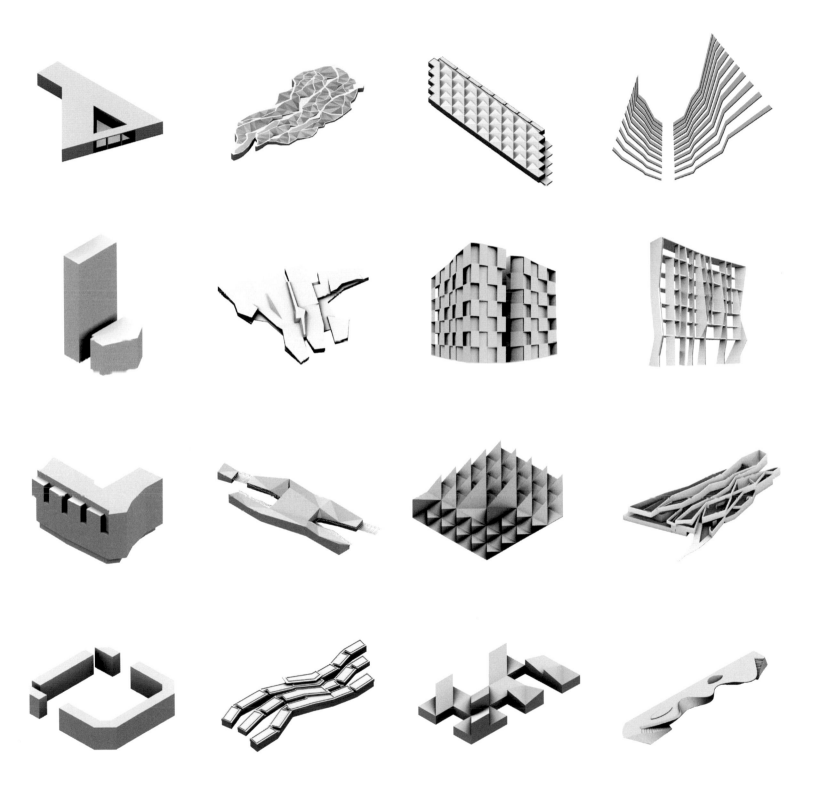

Landscape and geometry

Josep Maria Montaner

AA House is not one house; it is 4 houses

AA House by Carlos Ferrater and Xavier Martí is one of the most unique and intense single-family homes that has been built in recent times. It establishes a relationship with houses by Louis Khan, Alison and Peter Smithson, and Ray and Charles Eames.

Located in Sant Cugat, next to a forest bordering a golf course, the house rises from the road as a series of sloping roofs among the trees in the garden that form a magnificent belt of picturesque scenery.

On entering, the house greets us with a pool of water, an allegory of one of the four elements and born of a desire for reflections. Before entering, a totally austere plaza is defined. And upon entering, you discover a great longitudinal space, defined by skylights in the sloping roof. This great interior space is at once perfectly on a human scale.

The unique and unsettling fact that there appears to be no staircase and that none of the service facilities of the house are visible, all hidden away on a lower floor, leads us to believe this is not a house but something else; it is many houses at the same time. It is more of a pavilion than a house, given that the only thing to emerge is a large open level of rectangular panels in a bright white, as if it were a temporary Japanese pavilion or a marquee. The house is surrounded by grass, as if it were itself a form of plant life, and floats above it, taking on a mythical and imaginary image. It is reminiscent of the volumes of La Ricarda, the house by Antoni Bonet Castellana.

From the inside, rather than a house to stay in, it becomes a large camera. This sensation owes much to the orthogonal floor plan, perceived as diagonality and dynamicity; the cross section develops into inclined volumes capturing views of the landscaped garden and of the distant landscape beyond, incorporated into the landscape surrounding the house.

In short, it is more than a house, or even a pavilion or a camera; it is like a boat anchored in a green sea of grass. The stairs of this boat are what reveal this secret quality, hidden inside this light and airy house, which seems to be on the point of floating away. The four staircases leading to the lower domains are always hidden and always narrow, like those on a boat. A staircase beside the dining room and kitchen leads directly to the basement. There is a narrow staircase in the bedroom, which, also styled like those on a boat, leads between the walls directly down to the indoor swimming pool and sauna. A light and modern staircase goes from the library directly down to the cinema room, the space for fantasy and dreaming. Finally, there are service stairs leading down from the entrance, next to the kitchen, to the domestic staff apartment.

There are other stairs, also an important feature and, likewise, in the style of a boat, that go up to the higher levels, such as the lightweight contraption that unfolds like a ladder in the library and leads up to a loft where the owner's map collection is kept, the observatory of the world. The kitchen is another house, a world opened completely onto the garden and bathed in natural daylight, a systematic laboratory of nutrition, care, cleaning and work.

It is then that we discover the fourth house, which is the hidden house, the collector's house. It belongs to the collector of cars that are stored in the garage on the lower level. While the visible and representative house, after entering, next to the bar, is the large light-filled living area with piano and library at the back, the truly structuring space, the most private inner sanctum of the house, is not visible. It is the large garage belonging to the collector, where the permanent occupants of the house are to be found: cars, like machines of the subconscious, of desire, and of speed.

It is a house and it is the contrary: telluric and anchored at the base, and yet light and floating like a balloon about to leave the ground. It takes us back to the idea of a "house" as an authentic archetype as understood by Gaston Bachelard and Luís Barragán: with a basement and an attic. With all of its intensity and meaning, this house contains all the symbols. It is a house on pleasant land, all garden, which floats above the grass.

It is not a house. It is many houses. This is what makes it so unique, mythical, archetypal and unsettling. It is a world of illusions: it is a pavilion that floats on a green sea; it is a large camera to capture the surroundings in a thousand ways; it is a boat moored to the trees; it is a balloon about to take to the sky, anchored to the ground by a basement full of machines. it is, in short, the secret world dreamed of by two collectors.

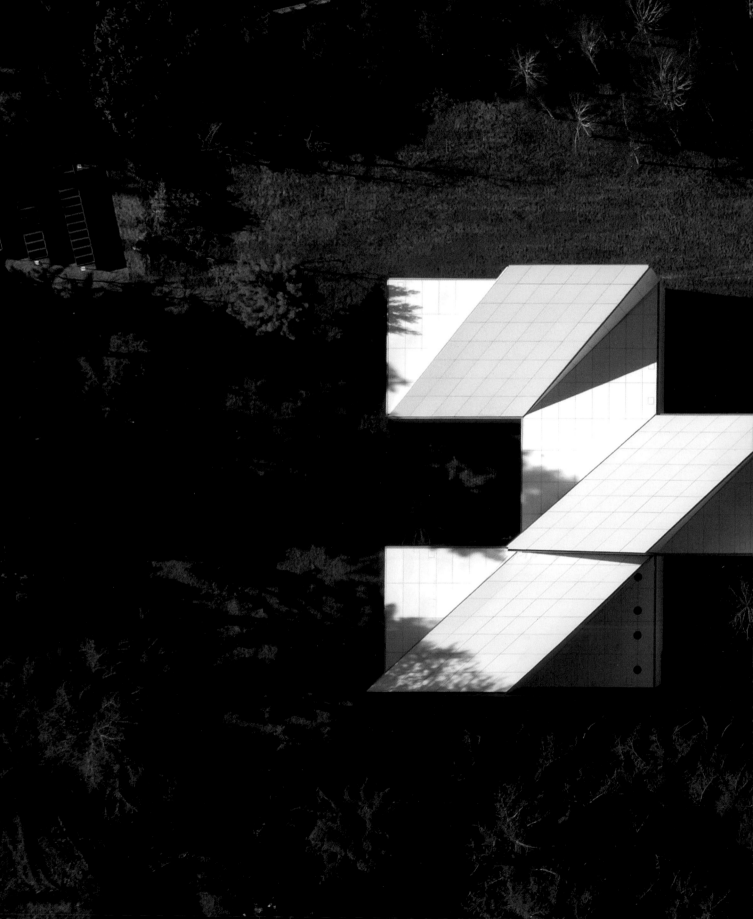

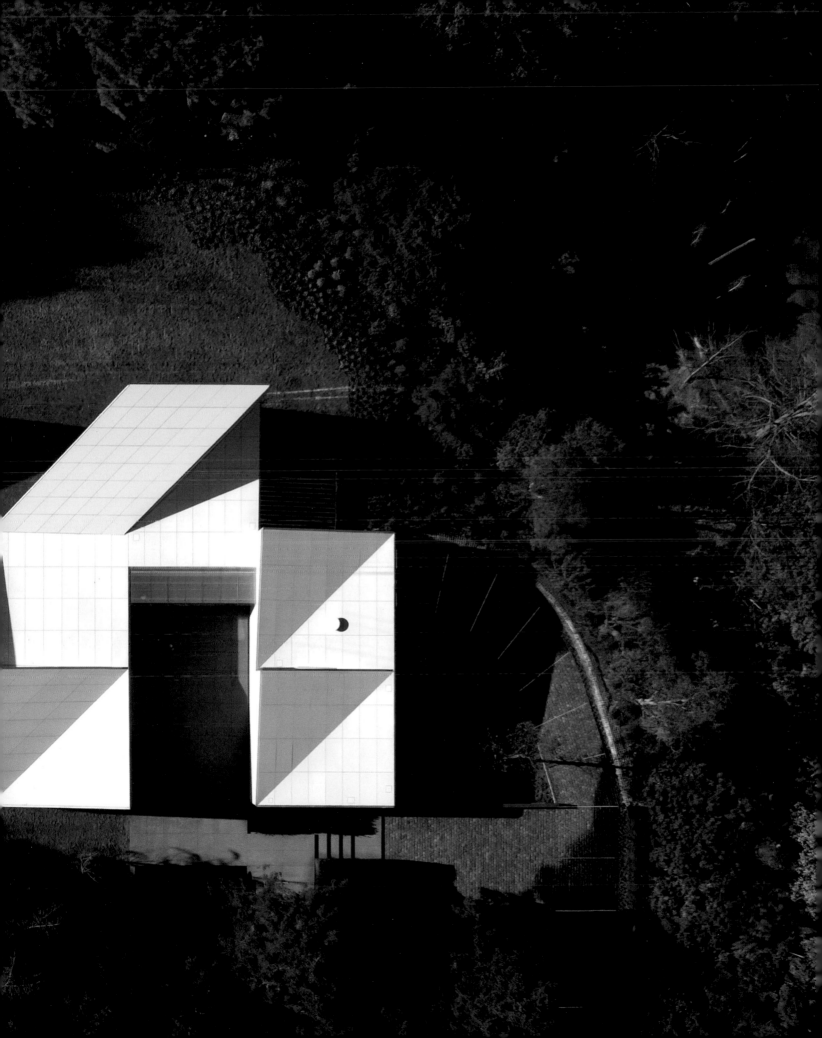

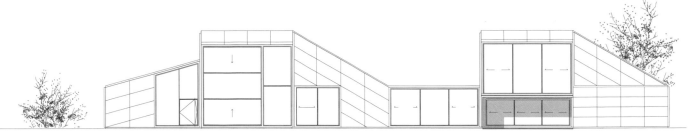

West elevation

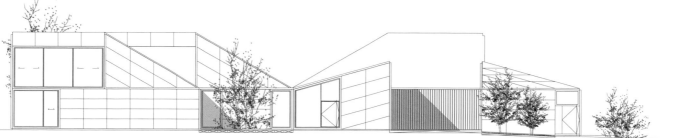

East elevation

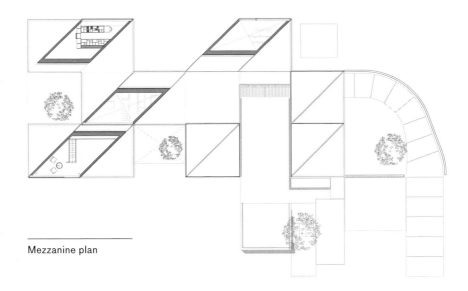

Mezzanine plan

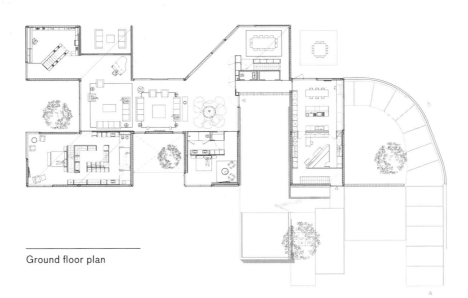

Ground floor plan

Basement floor plan

0 1 2   5

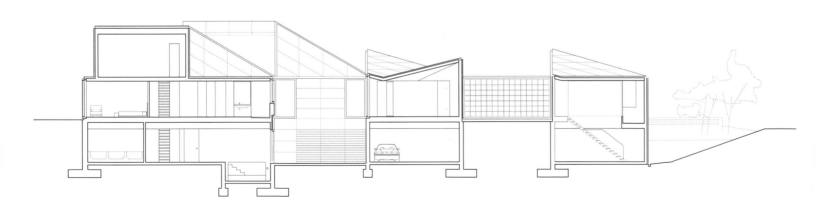

Longitudinal section

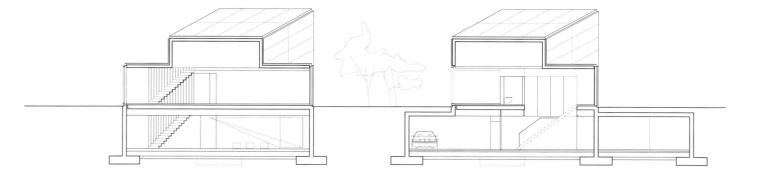

Cross section

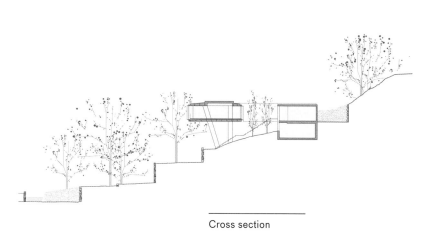

Cross section

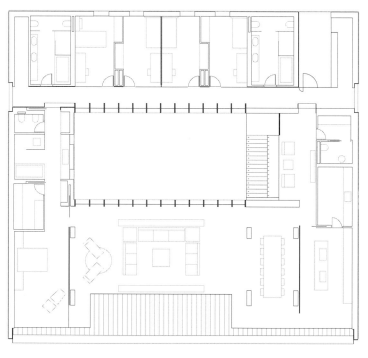

Ground floor plan

BF House

This home is on a plot of 3,000sqm with a height of 25m, in a Castellón neighborhood. Looking at the plot, we see that it reflectsits seventeenth century history, which is when overpopulation forced the cultivation of all types of terrain, including those that are very steep, through a system of small terraces with walls made of local rock. Our position towards the plot was that of absolute respect, so the construction method should also respect the land, thus us opting for a prefabricated building system that is deposited on the land practically without touching it, without cutting down trees, and taking advantage of existing terrace/garden areas.

Part of the house – garage and auxiliary areas – is buried, allowing us to re-introduce native vegetation on the natural terrain.

For construction, in trying to lessen the impact on the ground, we chose a metal structure fabricated in a workshop and transported to the site in large pieces that could be assembled.

An existing stone terrace supports the back part of the structure. This home looks as though suspended or in flight due to the dry construction materials used. The façade, resulting in various layers, is finished on the outside with corrugated sheet metal, specially designed to prevent glare and heat, thanks to the shadows caused by the folds. The great front opening is oriented towards magnificent views, and allows adequate sunlight in during the winter, but also protects from the sun in the summer. The solar energy panels with heat pipe technology on the roof allow the home to guarantee there will always be hot water available for both domestic use and for under-floor heating. Air currents cross the patio, taking advantage of the different orientations, which permits reductions in air conditioning consumption.

The intermediate courtyard allows access under the house, and at the same time, allows all the rooms to face the sun and the views. The whole house revolves around this courtyard.

East of the Mediterranean Sea

Cluster in Kaplankaya. Turkey

In the eastern Mediterranean, on the west coast of Turkey, facing the Greek islands, close to Bodrum, the ancient Halicarnassus, atop a headland 135 m above sea level, the new building is constructed in keeping with the fortresses, citadels, churches and monasteries that have characterized the landscape of the Mediterranean.

A banked wall of stone from the immediate vicinity delimits the geometric ground plan and the grounds themselves, helping the upper horizontal plane of the platform to merge with the natural topography, illuminated by patios and fissures in the wall, the complementary program of hammam, gymnasium and accesses to the upper platform.

Upon this platform, on a 40 x 40 meter-square ground plan with its axis on a north-south diagonal (the orientation of the Blue Mosque in Istanbul), there is a structure of screens, cantilevered girders and concrete pillars that go to form the skeleton of the building. A huge 6 m leave protects the ground-floor level beneath its shade, acting as a porch and intermediary space between inside and outside. On it, an intercolumniation of screens and pillars, along with huge roof lanterns, rounds the building off against the sky.

Within, an ample, off-center,double-height atrium is converted into the heart of the building: a place for exhibitions, encounters and celebrations. The different interiors—dining room, hall, library, cinema, assembly rooms—wrap around the great atrium on the ground floor, as, on the upper floor, do the apartmentsand the offices that complete the program. From this level, an open courtyard affords access to the upper viewing terrace.

The flexibility of its structure will have to enable different uses and demands to be accommodated over the course of time.

In its conception the intervention seeks after timelessness and permanence.

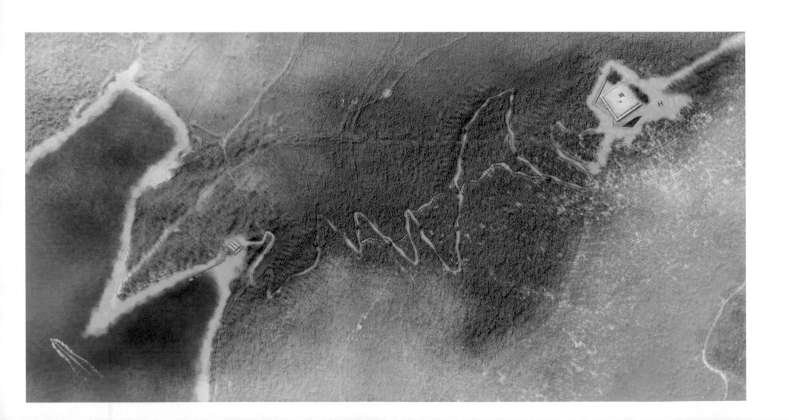

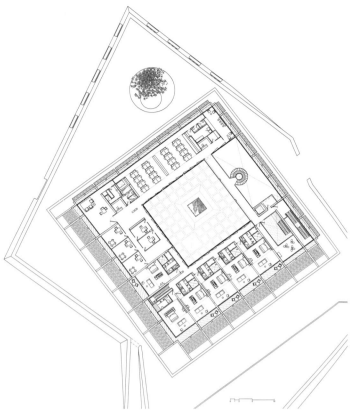

First floor plan

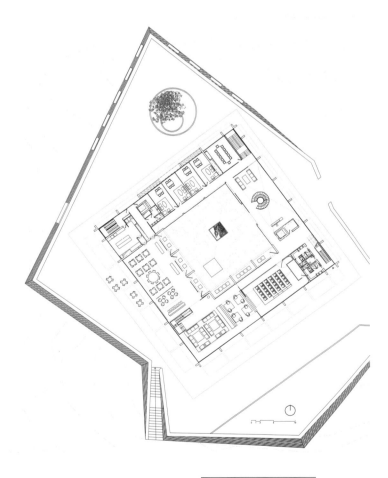

Ground floor plan

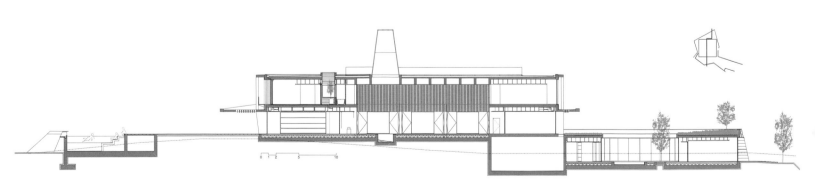

Section

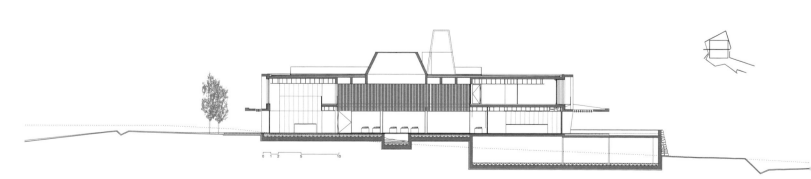

0 1 2   5   10

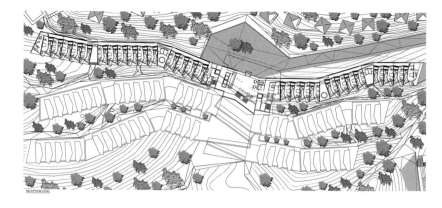

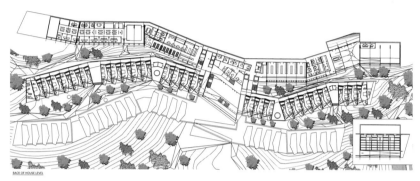

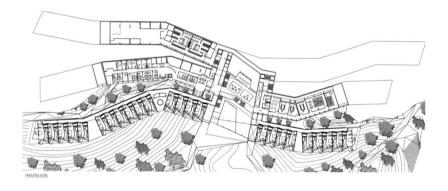

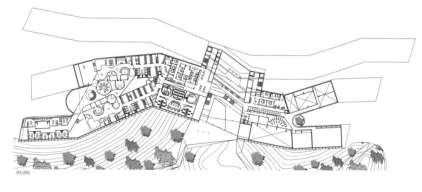

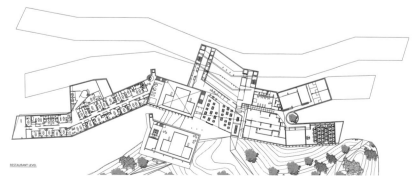

Six Senses Hotel in Bodrum. Turkey

We are not trying to urbanize a mountain, but to build a place for people. Arrive, leave, and return. That will be the condition of this new place. An identity based on a relationship with nature.

Utilizing similar rules for different units of activity: streets, piazzas, houses, landscape...- and taking advantage of the fractal geometric conditions of the landscape, new natural forms related to the Mediterranean paradigm appear.

The different buildings are finding accommodation in the topography, so many corners of the landscape become viewpoints from which to relate to the sea, sky and vegetation in an atmosphere of privacy and relaxation.

The hotel is situated in a privileged position. This facilitates the accessibility and logistics, as well as optimal relation with the bungalows and rental villas, which will complete the hotel. This privilege is most evident by its proximity to the sea and beaches.

The hotel is built on a new typology that hasn't existed to date; a configuration that, from the center, the functional program is organized and articulated by opened and closed spaces in the form of branches that adapt to the topography and create gaps that promote privacy, light, and quality views, ambience and landscape.

Thus Kaplankaya Six Senses recreates the imagery of the great resort, the underlying idea of the spa, and the romantic spirit of the great hotels of history, linked to landscape.

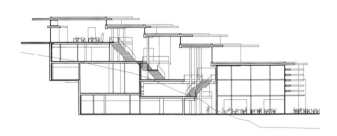

Hotel Section

Landscape
Section

OAB

Carlos Ferrater Lambarri Barcelona, 1944

Doctor of Architecture and Professor of Architectural Project Design at the Polytechnic University of Catalonia. Director of the Cátedra Blanca, Barcelona.

Academician-Elect of the *Real Academia de Belles Arts de Sant Jordi*.

Conferred as Doctor honoris causa by the University of Trieste.

In 2006 he set up, along with Xavier Martí, Lucía Ferrater and Borja Ferrater, the Office of Architecture in Barcelona (OAB), with Núria Ayala as Projects Director.

Awarded the 2009 National Architecture Award by the Spanish Ministry of Housing for his overall career and since december 2011 member of the Royal Institute of British Architects (International RIBA Felowship).

Gold Medal of the Fine Arts (Spain, 2019).

Since 2000 he has won five FAD Prizes, the 1999 and 2008 City of Barcelona Prize, the 2005 Brunel International Architecture Award (Denmark) and the 2009 BigMat Prize. He has three times been a finalist for the Mies van der Rohe Award. He has received the City of Madrid Award, the 2001 National Spanish Architecture Award, the 2006 Dedalo Minosse International Prize in Vicenza, the 2006 Decade Award and the 2007 International Flyer Award. The 2008 RIBA International Award was given to his Editorial MP monograph, among others. He received a mention in the X Biennial of Spanish Architecture and urbanism in 2009 and in the Urban Public Space European Award 2010 for the Benidorm Waterfront which also won the FAD 2010, Saloni Awards 2010, FOPA 2009, COACV 2007-2009 Award, the Chicago Athenaeum International Architecture Award "best global design" 2010 and the CEMEX 2011. In 2011 he had also received the National Spanish Architecture Prize with the Benidorm Waterfront. 1st Prize at the European Garden Award 2019/2020 for the Barcelona Botanical Garden. He was a guest exhibitor in the International Pavilion and the Spanish Pavilion at the 2004 Venice Biennale, and was invited by the MoMA, New York, to participate in the exhibition On-Site: New Architecture in Spain, and to exhibit his work in a one-man show at the Illinois Institute of Technology's Crown Hall in Chicago, the Bilbao Fine Arts Museum, the Israel Institute of Technology, the College of Architects of Catalonia, the Foundation of the College of Architects of Madrid and the Acquario Romano.

Beginning in June 2012, many models and original drawings of the Benidorm Waterfront have been chosen to form part of the collection of the Centre National d'Art et de Culture Georges Pompidou, along with the Iberia building on Paseo de Gracia and the Barcelona Botanical Garden. Some of them have been exhibited in the temporary Exhibition of the Pompidou "Modern Utopias" in Málaga. Also several original drawings are part of the Avery Collection of Columbia University.

Xavier Martí Galí Barcelona, 1969

Xavier Martí Galí graduated as an architect from the School of Architecture of Barcelona (ETSAB) in 1995.

He joined the Carlos Ferrater Studio as an associate architect in 2003. In 2006 he set up the Office of Architecture in Barcelona (OAB) with Carlos Ferrater, Lucía Ferrater and Borja Ferrater, with Núria Ayala as Projects Director.

He received the 2008 City of Barcelona Prize as co-designer of the Mediapro Tower in Barcelona.

For the Benidorm Waterfront he received the Spanish National Architecture Award 2011 for Urban design, 1st prize at CEMEX 2011 in the category of Infrastructure and Urban development, 2nd prize in International Sustainability and 3rd prize in International Accessibility WAN Award in Urban Design, HOSBEC Golden Insignia 2010, COACV Architecture Award 2007-2009 in the area of Urban Development and Landscaping, FAD Architecture Award 2010 in the category of City and Landscape, Chicago Athenaeum International Architecture Award "best new global design" 2010, Saloni Architecture Awards 2010, Fopa 2009 Prize for the work best integrated into the environment and respect for the environment, Applus Awards 2010, a special mention in the Urban Public Space European Award 2010, 8th ASCER Ceramic Awards 2009, Madrid Real Estate Salon Award 2006, ASPRIMA Award 2006 for the best tourist development and a place as a finalist in the "Rosa Barba" European Landscape Award 2010, as well as express recognition at the 9th Spanish Biennial of Architecture and Urban Development 2011.

In 2012 he received first prize at the Porcelanosa Awards for the BF House in Castellón.

As co-designer with Lucía Ferrater of the Casa Frente al Mar in Port de la Selva, he received the COAC Architecture Award 2017 and the 17th ASCER Ceramic Awards 2018.

He has given lectures in Spain, France, China, Mexico, Italy and Estonia. He was President of the Final Projects Tribunal at the La Salle School of Architecture in 2013 and President of the Court of the Enabling Master of the La Salle School of Architecture in 2010, as well as a member of the jury of several national and international architecture awards. In 2010 he was a guest professor on the Master's Degree in Projects XXI of the UPC.

Beginning in June 2012, many models and original drawings of the Benidorm Waterfront have been chosen to form part of the permanent collection of the Georges Pompidou National Centre for Art and Culture, with displays in Paris and Malaga.

Lucía Ferrater Barcelona, 1971

Borja Ferrater Barcelona, 1978

Lucía Ferrater graduated as an architect from the School of Architecture of Barcelona (ETSAB) in 1997.

In 1998 she joined the Carlos Ferrater studio as an associate architect.

In 2006 she helped set up the Office of Architecture in Barcelona (OAB), with Carlos Ferrater, Xavier Martí, Borja ferrater and Núria Ayala as Projects Director.

Her more important interventions in Barcelona are the refurbishing of the Coderch de Sentmenat house-studio in Plaça Calvó, a Social Services Center in the Eixample, and a housing complex in Plaça Lesseps. She has also designed an Evangelical church in Terrassa, various apartment and office buildings, two single-family houses, the Roca Barcelona Gallery, a hotel in Sitges and the Barcelona World Race Social Network. At present, she is working in the project of the Fish Market Building in Barcelona Port, a single-family house in Sitges (Barcelona), a 5* Hotel in Barcelona and several projects in the Tanger Harbor.

In 2006 she showed her Social Services Center in the Eixample of Barcelona at the MOMA, New York, in the exhibition On-Site: New Architecture in Spain.

She was a finalist in the 2000 FAD Prize for Architecture with an apartment building in Sant Cugat del Vallès.

2010 Wallpaper Design Award for Roca Barcelona Gallery building. COAC Award in 2017 and ASCER Award in 2019 for "Seafront House" in Port de la Selva.

She taught Projects of 5th and 6th-level Project Design at the International University of Catalonia's School of Architecture for three years. In 2012 she was teaching Projects in the Architectecture School of the European University of Madrid UEM. She was also teaching Projects at the ETSAB (UPC). At present she is 2th-level Projects teacher at the La Salle School of Architecture (URL) in Barcelona.

Collaborating professor annually at the Master MArch of Valencia. She has been Jury of the Cosentino Design Awards 2016 and the Neolith Awards 2017. She was a member of the jury of the 2013 Technal Palmarés Awards in Paris.

She is a member of the Board of Arquinfad association of the Fad (Promotion of the Arts and Design) and in the 2021 edition she has been a member of the Jury of the Fad Awards in the International category with Ricardo Bofill as president of the jury.

Between 1994-1997 he conducted studies in biology at Temple University (Philadelphia, PA, USA) and at the University of Navarra (Spain).

He is a licensed architect, graduating with Thesis Cum Laude in September 2005 from the International University of Catalonia (UIC). Project Skyscraper in Athens, Greece. Visiting Student at Sciarc, Los Angeles, US Dec. 2003. Participant at "Days of Oris Symposium 2005" Zagreb, Croatia

He has taught from January to June 2006 as both fourth-year course coordinator and Design Studio teacher at the International University of Catalonia (UIC). Being guest professor in the Workshop 'Emotional City' directed by British architects Sergison & Bates (Sept. 2006).

In January 2010, he got his Masters degree in Biodigital Architecture. He obtained his doctorate in April 2017 under the title "Use of complex Geometric Systems in Architectural Practice".

Between April 2008 and September 2011 Borja was Vice-Dean of Culture Publications and International Relations at the school of Architecture, ESARQ, UIC being also director of school workshops and lectures annual program. He was Visiting Assistant Professor during the 2011 spring semester in Pratt Institute, New York. He currently is teaching 3rd year Studio class at ESARQ UIC.

He is author of the book "Synchronizing Geometry" published by Actar, which has been exhibited at the Crown Hall of the IIT (Illinois Institute of Technology), Bezalel School of Arts, Jerusalem, Instituto Cervantes in Tel Aviv, Fine Arts Museum in Bilbao, At the Istanbul Institute of Architects and different art galleries in Madrid and Barcelona.

Founding Partner Architect of OAB (Office of Architecture in Barcelona) together with Xavier Marti, Carlos & Lucia Ferrater in January 2006. He is a FAD (Spain's national award) prize winner in the category of "ephemeral architecture" together with Carlos Ferrater for the exhibition in Madrid: "M.C. Escher El arte de lo impossible". Winner of Wallpaper* Design Awards 2010 for the building: Roca Barcelona Gallery together with Carlos and Lucía Ferrater. Recently, In may 2011 Borja also won the "Good Design is Good Business" awards organized by Architectural Record magazine with the RBG building. Also his work has been selected in the category 21 for 21 (for young architects) in WAN awards 2014. Borja was awarded with the international ENR magazine 2017 Best Global Project in the category of hospitality and Residential, with the project Kaplankaya Phase I Resort in Bodrum, Turkey. Recently his design for a 2*Michelin restaurant received the finalist award 2019 in the Spain & Portugal National FAD awards in the category of Interior Design.

He has given lectures, participated in round tables and jury of prizes in Sweden, Norway, Germany, USA, Mexico, UAE, Israel, UK, Sri Lanka, Japan, China, Malaysia, Australia, Turkey, Lebanon, Italy, Luxembourg, Andorra, Romania, and Spain. He has also had articles published about many of his works in multiple magazines, catalogues, and other publications.

Núria Ayala Prats Barcelona, 1975

Project Director

Núria Ayala graduated as an architect from the School of Architecture of Barcelona (ETSAB) in 2001.

She joined the Carlos Ferrater studio in 2000.

She is the Projects Director, collaborator and co-authorof different works, projects and competitions, including the NGO "Centre Esplai" (hostel, training facilities, offices and fitness center); the Musée des Confluences in Lyon; Casa Nolla; the GISA and FGC institutional Headquarters on Via Augusta in Barcelona; Las Palmas de Gran Canaria Promenade; the hotel in the Almodovar Gate in Cordoba; the Azahar Business Group Headquarters in Castellón; the new City Hall in Palma de Mallorca; the new IMQ Hospital in Bilbao; the development plan for the Garellano area of Bilbao; the La Seda Head Office in Barcelona; the City of Music in Sabadell; the extension to the Barcelona Botanical garden; the project design for Barcelona High Court; the extension to Torreblanca Park, Summer Camp NGO Viladoms, Club House in Bodrum – Turkey and Mixed use Buildings in the Miami Design Disctrict , Summer Camp NGO Rectoria de La Selva, two single family houses in Barcelona, an Office Building in Beirut, multihousing building and showroom Casa SEAT in Passeig de Gràcia 109-111 (Barcelona), NGO building expansión (hostel, multipurpose sports space and classrooms), Water Park at Prat del Llobregat (Barcelona), multifunctional building and music school NGO Polinyà (Barcelona).

Together with Carlos Ferrater she received, on 2010, Iberoamerican Biennial Architectural Prize, Ecola Prize and Finalist in Valencian Award for Azahar Business Group Headquarters.

On 2011, Finalist in the XI Spanish Biennial and Finalist in FAD Prize for Summer Camp NGO Viladoms.

She coordinated and did the graphic design for the "Research Process" in Sincronizar la geometría/ Synchronizing Geometry, published by Actar; Editorial MP's monograph Carlos Ferrater - OAB, the book "Casas y habitants" (Actar) and Actar's monograph "OAB. Office of Architecture in Barcelona"

Alberto Peñín Llobell, 1970

Architect

Architect since 1995, he is European PhD (2007) and chair professor at UPC where he teaches since 1999. Coordinator of master degree at ETSAB (MHIB) where he was vice dean (2014-17), director of the White Chair at UPC, and of ARIEN research group on Industry and Engineering, and Palimpsesto Magazine together with Carlos Ferrater. He was publisher of the book "Words with architects". With an extensive academic life as lecturer, design professor or master's teacher, he has participated in seminars, workshops or final diploma jury in Cooper Union (NY) and schools of architecture in Paris, Venice, Berlin, Monterrey, Milano, and several schools of Spain as Madrid, Valladolid, Sevilla, Toledo or Valencia.

He joined Peñín Architects in 1995, established in Valencia and Barcelona with special attention to urban and territorial design and, rehabilitation, housing and public buildings. His practice has been awarded with first price in around twenty professional competitions. His work, in buildings as "Centro del Imserso", "Aula Magna de Gandía" or "La Font d'en Carròs" School, has been selected at Young Architects of Spain, awarded at several occasions among which Valencia Order of Architects and Spanish and Latin American Bienal, and published at several professional magazines as Arquitectura Viva, ViA, AMC or C3. TC monograph "Peñín Arquitectos". AXA, Association member from its beginning in 2011.

Regular collaborator of Carlos Ferrater since 1997 and associated office of OAB since its creation in many works and projects in Spain, France, and Turkey. Among many projects and competitions made with OAB, he also built "Offices at Boulogne" (BEAU selection awards), "Vila-real library" (BIAU sel. awards), "Social houses" at Torrent and Castellón, Houses at Fernando Poo, Barcelona (FAD sel. awards), "Social Housing" at Toulouse (FAD sel.awards) and the "Union of Lawyers headquarters and offices" (Mies van der Rohe sel.awards).

Projects description

BALMES, 145
LOCATION: BARCELONA
DATE PROJECT: 2000 – REALIZATION: 2002
ARCHITECT: OAB. CARLOS FERRATER

BARCELONA BOTANICAL GARDEN – BOTANICAL INSTITUTE BUILDING - CSIC
LOCATION: MONTJUÏC, BARCELONA
PROMOTER: AJUNTAMENT DE BARCELONA
DATE PROJECT: 1995
REALIZATION: 1998-1999 (JBB)
PROJECT: 2000
REALIZATION: 2001-2003 (CSIC)
PROJECT: 2007
REALIZATION: 2007-2008 (EXTENSION)
ARCHITECT: OAB. CARLOS FERRATER
WITH J.L. CANOSA & BET FIGUERAS (PROJECT)
WITH JOAN GUIBERNAU – CSIC
WITH NÚRIA AYALA - EXTENSION 2007
WITH NÚRIA AYALA - MAINTENANCE
BUILDING 2015

VERTIX DIAGONAL BUILDING
LOCATION: CRISTOFOL DE MOURA ST/ BAC
DE RODA ST. BARCELONA
DATE PROJECT: 2003 –REALIZATION: 2007
ARCHITECT: OAB. CARLOS FERRATER,
XAVIER MARTÍ, C.PUEYO

LESSEPS M-3 BUILDING
LOCATION: C/ VELÁZQUEZ, C/ RIERA DE
VALLCARCA, BARCELONA
DATE PROJECT: 2004 – REALIZATION: 2008
ARCHITECT: OAB. CARLOS FERRATER –
LUCIA FERRATER – XAVIER MARTÍ

**TWELVE HOUSES IN C/ FERNANDO POO
C/ SANT FRANCESC**
LOCATION: BARCELONA
DATE PROJECT: 2015 – REALIZATION 2016-2018
ARCHITECT: OAB. CARLOS FERRATER –
XAVIER MARTÍ / ALBERTO PEÑÍN

CARTAGENA, 312
LOCATION: BARCELONA
DATE PROJECT: 2017 – REALIZATION 2018-2019
ARCHITECT: OAB. CARLOS FERRATER –
LUCIA FERRATER

INTERMODAL STATION "ZARAGOZA-DELICIAS"
LOCATION: ZARAGOZA
DATE PROJECT: 1999 – REALIZATION 2001-2003
ARCHITECT: OAB.CARLOS FERRATER / JOSE
M. VALERÓ WITH FELIX ARRANZ – ELENA MATEU

**INTERMODAL BUILDING OF BARCELONA
AIRPORT**
LOCATION: AEROPUERTO DE EL PRAT.
BARCELONA
DATE PROJECT: 2002 – REALIZATION 2007
ARCHITECT: OAB. C. FERRATER / R. SANABRIA
J.M. CASADEVALL

ROSSELLÓ, 257
LOCATION: BARCELONA
DATE PROJECT: 2015 – REALIZATION 2015-2017
ARCHITECT: OAB. CARLOS FERRATER –
LUCIA FERRATER

MULTIHOUSING BUILDING IN BARCELONA
LOCATION: PASSEIG DE GRÀCIA, 99
DATE PROJECT: 2004
REALIZATION 2005-2007
ARCHITECT: OAB. CARLOS FERRATER –
LUCÍA FERRATER WITH JOAN GUIBERNAU &
ELENA MATEU

MULTIHOUSING BUILDING IN BARCELONA
LOCATION: PASSEIG DE GRÀCIA, 23 –
DIPUTACIÓ, 259
DATE PROJECT: 1996 – REALIZATION 1999
ARCHITECT: OAB. CARLOS FERRATER / JOAN
GUIBERNAU WITH XAVIER MARTÍ GALÍ

HOTEL MANDARIN IN BARCELONA
LOCATION: PASSEIG DE GRÀCIA, 38-40.
BARCELONA
DATE PROJECT: 2007 – REALIZATION 2010
ARCHITECT: OAB. CARLOS FERRATER /
JUAN TRIAS DE BES

PASSEIG DE GRÀCIA, 30
LOCATION: BARCELONA
DATE PROJECT: 2004
ARCHITECT: OAB. CARLOS FERRATER –
XAVIER MARTÍ / JUAN TRÍAS DE BES

PASSEIG DE GRÀCIA, 109-111
LOCATION: PG. GRÀCIA 109-111 / AVDA.
DIAGONAL. BARCELONA
DATE PROJECT: 2017
REALIZATION: CASA SEAT: 2018-2020
MULTI-HOUSING TOWER: 2019-2022
ARCHITECT: OAB. CARLOS FERRATER – WITH
XAVIER MARTÍ AND NÚRIA AYALA

PASSEIG DE GRÀCIA, 125-127
LOCATION: BARCELONA
DATE PROJECT: 2015 – REALIZATION: 2016-2019
ARCHITECT: OAB. CARLOS FERRATER –
XAVIER MARTÍ

SCIENCE PARK IN GRANADA
LOCATION: AV. DEL MEDITERRANEO, S/N
DATE PROJECT: 2004 – REALIZATION 2005-2008
ARCHITECT: OAB. C.FERRATER / E. JIMENEZ,
Y. BRASA

MULTIHOUSING BUILDING IN BILBAO
LOCATION: EUSKADI SQ, BILBAO
DATE PROJECT: 2005 – REALIZATION
2007-2011
ARCHITECT: OAB. C. FERRATER – X. MARTÍ –
L. FERRATER / L. DOMÍNGUEZ

IMQ HOSPITAL
LOCATION: DEUSTO, BILBAO
DATE PROJECT: 2009 – REALIZATION 2010-2012
ARCHITECT: OAB. CARLOS FERRATER –
ALFONSO CASARES WITH NÚRIA AYALA,
A. OCAÑA, L. DOMÍNGUEZ

AQUILEIA TOWER
LOCATION: JESOLO, VENECIA, ITALY
DATE PROJECT: 2004 – REALIZATION: 2009
ARCHITECT: OAB. CARLOS FERRATER /
GUSTAVO CARABAJAL WITH XAVIER MARTÍ GALÍ

**NGO CENTRE ESPLAI / NGO VILADOMS /
NGO RECTORIA**
LOCATION: EL PRAT DE LLOBREGAT /
CASTELLBELL I EL VILAR / NAVÈS
DATE PROJECT: CENTRE ESPLAI 2006 –
REALIZATION 2006-2007
PROJECT VILADOMS 2009 – REALIZATION 2010
PROJECT RECTORIA 2014 – REALIZATION 2015
ARCHITECT: OAB. CARLOS FERRATER –
NÚRIA AYALA

THE AZAHAR GROUP HEADQUARTERS
LOCATION: CARRETERA NACIONAL 340.
CASTELLÓN
DATE PROJECT: 2004 – REALIZATION: 2009
ARCHITECT: OAB. CARLOS FERRATER –
NÚRIA AYALA

REGINA HOUSE
LOCATION: GAUSES, VILOPRIU (GIRONA)
DATE PROJECT 2018 – REALIZATION
2019-2020
ARCHITECT: OAB. CARLOS FERRATER

ALENTI HOTEL
LOCATION: INDUSTRIA SQ.- 1er DE MAIG. SITGES
DATE PROJECT: 2007 – REALIZATION: 2009
ARCHITECT: OAB. CARLOS FERRATER –
LUCÍA FERRATER

**UNITED EVANGELICAL CHURCH IN
BARCELONA**
LOCATION: BÉJAR AV. TERRASSA
DATE PROJECT: 2007 – REALIZATION
2008-2010
ARCHITECT: OAB. CARLOS FERRATER –
LUCÍA FERRATER

BARCELONA WORLD RACE
LOCATION: BARCELONA'S PORT
DATE PROJECT: 2010 – REALIZATION: 2010
ARCHITECT: OAB. C. FERRATER –
L. FERRATER / J.CARBONELL

MICHELIN HEADQUARTERS BUILDING
LOCATION: ZAC SEGUIN RIVES DE SEINE -
BOULOGNE
DATE PROJECT: 2007 – REALIZATION: 2010
ARCHITECT: OAB. C. FERRATER / E.BABIN
F. RENAUD – A.PEÑIN

MULTI HOUSING IN TOULOUSE
LOCATION: TOULOUSE
DATE PROJECT ZAC ANDROMEDE: 2013
REALIZATION: 2013-2016
PROJECT ZAC MONGES: 2012
REALIZATION: 2013-2018
ARCHITECT: OAB. C. FERRATER – XAVIER
MARTÍ / ALBERTO PEÑÍN

LAWYERS UNION HEADQUARTERS
LOCATION: LYON (FRANCE)
DATE PROJECT: 2014 – REALIZATION 2015-2018
ARCHITECT: OAB. C. FERRATER / A. PEÑÍN /
B. DUMETIER

VILA REAL PUBLIC LIBRARY
LOCATION: VILA REAL, CASTELLON
DATE PROJECT: 2009 – REALIZATION
2009-2011
ARCHITECT: OAB. C. FERRATER / ALBERTO
PEÑIN WITH J. GIMENO

MEDIAPRO BUILDING
LOCATION: DIAGONAL AV. 177-183, 22@
DISTRICT, BARCELONA
DATE PROJECT: 2005 – REALIZATION: 2008
ARCHITECT: OAB. CARLOS FERRATER /
PATRICK GENARD WITH XAVIER MARTI GALÍ
STRUCTURE: JUAN CALVO (PONDIO)

**CORPORATE HEADQUARTERS FOR GISA
AND FGC**
LOCATION: VIA AUGUSTA – VERGOS ST.
BARCELONA
DATE PROJECT: 2006 – REALIZATION: 2009
ARCHITECT: OAB. CARLOS FERRATER –
NÚRIA AYALA

HIPÓDROMO TOWER
LOCATION: AVDA.PATRIA-AVDA.
HIPÓDROMO–GUADALAJARA (MEXICO)
DATE PROJECT: 2013 – REALIZATION: 2015
ARCHITECT: OAB. CARLOS FERRATER –
XAVIER MARTÍ

ROCA BARCELONA GALLERY
LOCATION: CALLE JOAN GÜELL 211, BARCELONA
DATE PROJECT: 2008 – REALIZATION: 2009
ARCHITECT: OAB. B. FERRATER – C. FERRATER
L. FERRATER

**COCINA HERMANOS TORRES
RESTAURANT**
LOCATION: C/ TAQUÍGRAF SERRA, 20.
BARCELONA
DATE PROJECT: 2018 – REALIZATION: 2018
ARCHITECT: OAB. CARLOS FERRATER –
BORJA FERRATER

BENIDORM WEST BEACH PROMENADE
LOCATION: BENIDORM. ALICANTE
DATE PROJECT: 2002 – REALIZATION:
2006-2009
ARCHITECT: OAB. CARLOS FERRATER –
XAVIER MARTÍ GALÍ
STRUCTURE: JUAN CALVO (PONDIO)

TANGIER WATERFRONT
LOCATION: TANGIER. MOROCCO
DATE PROJECT: 2013 – REALIZATION:
2014-2017
ARCHITECT: OAB. CARLOS FERRATER –
XAVIER MARTÍ – LUCÍA FERRATER

THE BARCELONA FISHMARKET
LOCATION: BARCELONA'S PORT
DATE PROJECT: 2012 – IN PROGRESS
ARCHITECT: OAB. C. FERRATER –
L. FERRATER / J. COLL

**"HORIZONSCRAPER" IN THE SEAFRONT
OF BARCELONA**
LOCATION: BARCELONA'S WATERFRONT
DATE PROJECT: 2014
ARCHITECT: OAB. CARLOS FERRATER

108 SOCIAL HOUSING
LOCATION: JOSEP TARRADELLAS /
Av. L'HOSPITALET. BARCELONA
DATE PROJECT: 2012 – REALIZATION:
2013-2014
ARCHITECT: OAB. CARLOS FERRATER –
NURIA AYALA WITH CC245. SERGI BLANCH,
SANDRA RODÀ

**SOCIAL HOUSING JOSÉ PÉREZ IN
VILLAVERDE**
LOCATION: CTRA. VILLAVERDE – JOSÉ
PÉREZ. MADRID
DATE PROJECT: 2002 – REALIZATION:
2002-2005
ARCHITECT: CARLOS FERRATER

HOUSE IN ALCANAR
LOCATION: CASAS DE ALCANAR. TARRAGONA
DATE PROJECT: 2003 – REALIZATION: 2006
ARCHITECT: OAB. CARLOS FERRATE WITH
CARLOS ESCURA

SEAFRONT HOUSE
LOCATION: PORT DE LA SELVA (GIRONA)
DATE PROJECT: 2013 – REALIZATION:
2014-2016
ARCHITECT: OAB. XAVIER MARTÍ –
LUCÍA FERRATER

PINEDA HOUSE
LOCATION: BARCELONA
DATE PROJECT: 2014 – REALIZATION:
2014-2016
ARCHITECT: OAB. BORJA FERRATER –
LUCÍA FERRATER

**L'ESCALA SEAFRONT AND
REFURBISHMENT OF A PARENT'S HOUSE**
LOCATION: L'ESCALA (GIRONA)
DATE PROJECT SEAFRONT: 2014 –
REALIZATION: 2015-2017
PROJECT REFURBISHMENT 2012 –

REALIZATION. 2013
ARCHITECT: OAB. CARLOS FERRATER

AA HOUSE – ORIGAMI HOUSE
LOCATION: BARCELONA
DATE PROJECT: 2007-2009
ARCHITECT: OAB CARLOS FERRATER –
XAVIER MARTÍ

BF HOUSE
LOCATION: URB. LA COMA. BORRIOL.
CASTELLÓN
DATE PROJECT: 2006 – REALIZATION: 2011
ARCHITECT: OAB. CARLOS FERRATER –
XAVIER MARTÍ GALÍ
ADI. CARLOS ESCURA - CARLOS MARTIN

THE BARCELONA EDITION HOTEL
LOCATION: AVDA. CAMBÓ 14, BARCELONA
DATE PROJECT: 2014 – REALIZATION:
2015–2018
ARCHITECT: OAB. CARLOS FERRATER –
XAVIER MARTÍ GALÍ

HOTEL SEVENTY
LOCATION: CÒRSEGA, 344. BARCELONA
DATE PROJECT: 2012 – REALIZATION:
2013–2018
ARCHITECT: OAB. CARLOS FERRATER –
XAVIER MARTÍ GALÍ

THE STANDARD IBIZA HOTEL
LOCATION: VARA DEL REY. IBIZA
DATE PROJECT: 2017 – REALIZATION:
2017–2020
ARCHITECT: OAB. C. FERRATER –
B. FERRATER – L. FERRATER

CLUSTER KAPLANKAYA IN BODRUM
LOCATION: MUGLA. BODRUM. TURKEY
DATE PROJECT: 2011 – REALIZATION:
2012–2013
ARCHITECT: OAB. CARLOS FERRATER –
BORJA FERRATER

SIX SENSES HOTEL IN BODRUM
LOCATION: MUGLA. BODRUM. TURKEY
DATE PROJECT: 2012 – REALIZATION:
2012–2016
ARCHITECT: OAB. C.FERRATER –
B. FERRATER / J. TRIAS DE BES

INSTANT CITY
LOCATION: CALA SAN MIGUEL. IBIZA
DATE REALIZATION: SET – OCT 1961
ARCHITECT: CARLOS FERRATER –
FERNANDO BENDITO WITH JOSÉ MIGUEL DE
PRADA-POLE
PHOTOGRAFER: JOSÉ MANUEL FERRATER

MENORCA GUESTS PAVILION
LOCATION: SON AÏET. CIUTADELLA.
MENORCA
DATE PROJECT: 1992 – REALIZATION:
1995-1998
ARCHITECT: CARLOS FERRATER

CARLOS FERRATER 1991-2005
WWW.FERRATER.COM

Carlos Ferrater work from 1970 to 2005

The career of Carlos Ferrater (1944) got under way in the context of a an outdated modernism. His first piece of work, 54 dwellings in the Sant Just Park housing complex in Sant Just Desvern, was rooted in the oeuvre of José Antonio Coderch: it announced a recurrent wish for realism, for efficiency, for tempered rationalism adapted to the context. The apartment buildings in Barcelona's Calle Bertrán were demonstrations of his ability to progress in terms of typological invention. These early buildings, with its abstraction and its transparency, could be brought into line with Mediterranean classicism. This same period witnessed have recourse to the lightness of pavilions in which mass dematerialized, the inspiration being the architecture of Mies van der Rohe, as shown by the sports pavilion in Torroella de Montgrí. And that first phase culminated in the Guix de la Meda house, the Garbí building and the design for the Yatch Club in L'Estartit.

The boom prior to the Olympic Games was a busy time for Ferrater, as his team took on a number of projects that were highly representative of Olympic Barcelona: the three city blocks in the Olympic Village, the dwellings in Vall d'Hebron, the Hotel Juan Carlos I (1988-92), and the Botanical Garden, the competition for which he won in 1989. His two great urban undertakings to do with communal housing. This volumetric forcefulness led to the creation of almost intimate open spaces inside the city block, thus endowing public space.

Following the Olympic period, the possibility arose for new experiments like the "minimalism" of the IMPIVA in Castellón and the introduction of fractal forms, first developed in the Fitness Center for the Hotel Juan Carlos I. Ferrater's team made two further experiments: the studio-house for a photographer in Llampaies and the Arruga Film Studios in Sant Just Desvern. And the period concluded with the Convention Center on the Diagonal.

Prior to the creation in 2005 of OAB (Office of Architecture in Barcelona), some of the practice's most representative buildings were completed and highly regarded works as the block in Roger de Flor, the Ibiza's House, the new El Prat Royal Golf Club or the International JC Decaux Headquarters. This period culminated with the Castellon Auditorium Center.

Josep Maria Montaner. Historian and Professor of Composition

Instant City 1971. Photo: J.M. Ferrater

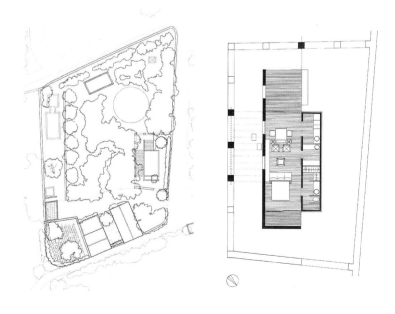

In the summer of 1972, after the Instant City experiment the previous year in Cala San Miquel in the north of Ibiza, we sailed to Minorca from Estartit in an old traditional llaüt and got to know the island. From then Minorca was the backdrop for idyllic family holidays, first of all in the summer with our successive sailing boats, until in 1991 we began renovating some old Boers in Son Aiet, on the road leading to the southern beaches very near to Ciutadella.

In time, that idyllic place – an area of orchards, dry stone walls and sandstone marker posts – became the refuge for family and friends: a home from home. There, I have been able to do some of my best work, prepare for competitive examinations and produce books such as Casas and Habitantes. It was also there, in the first decade of the 2000s, that OAB was conceived, and it became the scene of family events, meetings and gatherings with many guests and visitors. It is a place where work and leisure have been mixed, where time takes on another value, and where silence competes with the noise of the grandchildren.

Carlos Ferrater

Port d'Estartit 1979

Guix de la Meda 1984

Sport pavilion in Torroella 1982

Sant Just Park 1974

Bertràn 67 1981

Triginer house 1993

Fitness centre 1996

IMPIVA headquarters 1995

LOLA Restaurant 1992

Hotel in Avinguda Diagonal 1992

Catalunya Congress Centre 2000

Olympic Village in Poblenou 1992

House in Molinet 1986

Garbí building 1988

Nautical club Estartit 1991

Golf club el Prat 1999

Empordà Golf Club Hotel 2003

Social centre 2001

House in Llampaies 1993

School in Lloret de Mar 1996

Tagomago house 1999

Olympic Village in Vall d'Hebrón 1991

International Decaux 2001

Auditorium building in Castelló 2004

El Nou Jardí Botànic de Barcelona 1989

Tres mansanes vora la Vila Olimpica 1989

Documentos de Arquitectura 1989

Carlos Ferrater. Introducción W.Curtis 1998

Building a Public Building 1999

Carlos Ferrater 2000

Materialidad 2003

2G 2004

Carlos Ferrater OAB 2006

Casas y Habitantes 2008

Parque de las Ciencias de Granada 2008

Synchronizing and Geometry 2006

OAB Office of Architecture (Vol. I) 2015

Kaplankaya Club House 2015

Casas. Internacional 2019

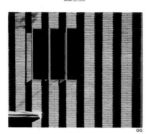

Catálogos de Arquitectura Contemporánea 1989

Carlos Ferrater. Ignasi de Solà Morales 1995

Materiality 1997

Carlos Ferrater 2000

Más grueso que el papel 2000

TC Cuadernos, Valencia 2002

Kaplankaya 2007

Carlos Ferrater. Opere e Progetti (Vol. I) 2007

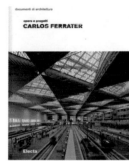

Carlos Ferrater. Opere e Progetti (Vol. II) 2007

Carlos Ferrater & Partners 2010

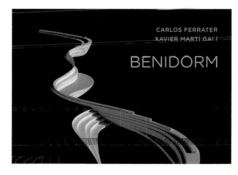

Benidorm 2011

Casa AA / Origami House 2012

Cocinas Hermanos Torres Restaurant 2019

Geometric Taxonomy 2021

www.ferrater.com

Published by
ACTAR
New York_Barcelona
www.actar.com

Edited by
Carlota Aluja
Núria Ayala

Text supervision
Borja Ferrater

Translation
Paul Hammond
Simon Berrill

Graphic design and production
Actar Publishers

Graphic documentation
Estudio OAB

OAB Archive
Gisela Folch

Photographs
OAB would like to thank the
photographers who have shot our
work, especially Aleix Bagué and
Joan Guillamat

Aleix Bagué 10, 12a, 15-19, 22,
23a, 25-29,36-38, 41, 43, 48-
49, 51-57, 64-65, 70, 71, 73b, 74-
75, 80a, 81, 86, 94-95, 100-107,
127-129, 133-139, 142-151, 162-
165, 178-181, 183-193, 196-203,
206-209, 218-231, 236-239,
242-243, 254-255, 259-263,
268-271, 276-277, 282, 284-297,
349, 300-301

Joan Guillamat 12b, 23b, 24, 30-
33, 35, 39, 44-47, 66-69, 74,
83-85, 87-91, 109-115, 126, 130-
131, 140, 141, 154-155, 160-161,
170-177, 194-195, 212-217, 240-
241, 244-245, 249-253, 257,
266, 273, 275, 278, 303-317,
319, 321-339, 341-343, 351

Dani Rovira 11, 76-79, 166-167,169
Alessandra Chemollo 118-125
Lluís Casals 72, 73a, 158
Juan Rodríguez 156-157, 298-299

U.S ISBN: 978-1-638400-16-5
PCN, Library of Congress Control
Number: 2022931954

Printing and bound
in the European Union

Distribution
Actar Distribution
New York_Barcelona
www.actar.com

New York
440 Park Avenue South,
17th Floor
NEW YORK, NY 10016, USA
T +1 2 129 662 207
salesnewyork@actar-d.com

Barcelona
Roca i Batlle 2-4
08023 BARCELONA, Spain
T +34 933 282 183
eurosales@actar-d.com

OAB
Office of Architecture
in Barcelona